ASIANISING
SINGAPORE

The Institute of Southeast Asian Studies was established as an autonomous organisation in May 1968. It is a regional research centre for scholars and other specialists concerned with modern Southeast Asia, particularly the multi-faceted problems of stability and security, economic development, and political and social change.

The Institute is governed by a twenty-two-member Board of Trustees comprising nominees from the Singapore Government, the National University of Singapore, the various Chambers of Commerce, and professional and civic organisations. A ten-man Executive Committee oversees day-to-day operations; it is chaired by the Director, the Institute's chief academic and administrative officer.

The responsibility for facts and opinions expressed in this publication rests exclusively with the author; his interpretation does not necessarily reflect the views or the policy of the Institute.

ASIANISING SINGAPORE

The PAP's Management of Ethnicity

RAJ VASIL

*Issued under the auspices of the
Institute of Southeast Asian Studies*

HEINEMANN ASIA
Singapore

Published by
Heinemann Asia, a Division of
Reed Elsevier (Singapore) Pte Ltd
Consumer/Education Books
37 Jalan Pemimpin, #07-04/05, Block B
Union Industrial Building
Singapore 577177

OXFORD LONDON EDINBURGH MELBOURNE SYDNEY
AUCKLAND MADRID ATHENS IBADAN NAIROBI
GABORONE HARARE KINGSTON PORTSMOUTH (NH)

All rights reserved. No part of this publication may be reproduced, stored in a retrieval system, or transmitted in any form or by any means, electronic, mechanical, photocopying, recording or otherwise, without the prior permission of Heinemann Asia.

ISBN 9971-64-456-8

© Raj Vasil 1995
First published 1995

Cover photograph courtesy of Singapore Tourist Promotion Board
Typeset by Linographic Services Pte Ltd (11/13pt Berkeley Book)
Printed in Singapore by Utopia Press

For Gary Hawke,

in friendship

CONTENTS

List of Tables ... viii

Preface ... ix

CHAPTER 1
Introduction ... 1

CHAPTER 2
Singapore in Malaysia: 1963–65 ... 8

CHAPTER 3
Cultural Democracy:
   The Founding Principle ... 18

CHAPTER 4
Managing Ethnic Diversity:
   The First Phase, 1965–79 ... 38
   Creating an English-Speaking Singapore ... 52

CHAPTER 5
Asianising Singapore:
   The Second Phase, 1979–90 ... 64

CHAPTER 6
Management of Ethnicity: Since 1990 ... 99
   Asianising Singapore ... 113
   Ameliorating Inter-Ethnic Disparities ... 136
   Maintaining a National Consensus on the
      Management of Ethnicity ... 152

INDEX ... 158

LIST OF TABLES

CHAPTER 1

Table 1:	Population of Singapore, by Race, 1871–1990	2
Table 2:	Religious Affiliations, 1980 and 1990	4
Table 3:	Predominant Household Language by Racial Group, 1980 and 1990	5

CHAPTER 3

Table 4:	Economic Indicators, 1972 and 1982	36

CHAPTER 4

Table 5:	School Enrolments, 1959, 1972 and 1985	59
Table 6:	Primary School Enrolments, 1972 and 1982	59

CHAPTER 6

Table 7:	Working Persons Aged Fifteen and over by Monthly Income and Ethnic Group, 1980 and 1990	141
Table 8:	Number of Households by Type of Dwelling, 1980 and 1990	142
Table 9:	Students by Level of Education, 1980 and 1990	142
Table 10:	Occupational Distribution of Workforce, 1980 and 1990	143
Table 11:	Progress Achieved by Malays, 1981 and 1991	144

PREFACE

This study is an overview of the successful management of ethnicity in Singapore by two generations of its People's Action Party rulers. Looking around the world today and watching the viciousness and savagery of ethnic conflict, it is not unreasonable to say that today's Singapore stands as the most monumental achievement of its rulers and its people. It bears reminding Singaporeans that their economic miracle would not have been possible without that. What Singapore could be today, but for the sagacity of its rulers as well as its citizens, should be a cause for sober reflection.

It is to the credit of the PAP rulers that they have not allowed themselves to be overly influenced by the fact that more than three-quarters of Singapore's population has consisted of the Chinese. They chose, and throughout adhered to, the concept of cultural democracy as the founding principle of the Singapore state which allowed the distinctively different ethnic components of the island's population cultural autonomy and a role and status as persons and communities of equal worth. Where else in the world today can one see the good sense of politics continue to prevail over the absurd arrogance of economics, especially in these days of the magic of the market, the paramountcy of private enterprise and the utter fairness of user pay? Covering an area only of 640 square kilometres, with a population of no more than 2.5 million, the city state continues ("wastefully") to use four official languages, including Tamil which is the language of less than five per cent of its population.

The PAP rulers also built up such a high degree of credibility as *national* leaders, not being especially beholden to any one particular ethnic segment, that they have been able to adapt and modify the founding principle of cultural democracy when required, to suit the interests of Singapore and its changing realities without having to worry excessively about the political costs involved. It is reflected in their being able to manage smoothly, during the past three decades, dramatic change from an ethnically fragmented and separated Singapore to an essentially English-speaking Singapore to an Asianising Singapore. Credit must also be given to the different peoples of Singapore, all of whom may not always have acted as angels, for showing a sense of responsibility and political maturity strong enough to enable their rulers to adhere steadfastly to their commitment to a multi-cultural Singaporean Singapore.

I am deeply grateful to many in Singapore, who during the past three decades willingly talked with me. Unfortunately, most of them have to remain nameless because this was the basis on which they shared their thoughts and feelings with me. I owe a special debt of gratitude to Prime Minister Goh Chok Tong who has always kindly found time to talk and share his views with me with exceptional frankness. My grateful thanks to my friend, Lau Teik Soon, for all his help and hospitality. I am also thankful to the Institute of Southeast Asian Studies, where I was an ISEAS Research Fellow during the preparation of this study.

Raj Vasil
Victoria University of Wellington

CHAPTER 1

Introduction

Historically, the small island state of Singapore, covering an area of some 640 square kilometers only, had always been a part of Malaya. However, in 1819, Stamford Raffles, on behalf of the British, established it as a separate economic and political entity. A few years later, in 1826, it was joined by the British with their nearby possessions, Malacca and Penang, to form the Straits Settlements which, from 1867, came to be ruled directly by the British government. With that began remarkable economic expansion and growth, and it did not take long before Singapore was turned into the foremost centre of trade and commerce in the Southeast Asian region. The immense new economic opportunities offered by the island attracted vast numbers of immigrants from China, India and the neighbouring Malay countries. Soon a dynamic, hard-working and exceedingly diverse multi-racial society was created, although it remained predominantly Chinese.

Later, after the British had begun to rule Malaya on behalf of its traditional Malay rulers, they sought to merge Singapore with Malaya in order to secure the island's economic future. However, the British were unable to effect the merger because of the vehement opposition to the idea by the Malay rulers of the nine Malay states that constituted British Malaya. The Malay rulers were fearful, firstly, that it would inevitably turn their "sovereign" states into a colony directly ruled by the British, and secondly, that it would alter the racial balance of population in a way

Table 1: *Population of Singapore, by Race, 1871–1990*

(number and per cent)

	1871	1911	1947	1970	1990
Malays	26,148	46,952	115,735	311,379	380,600
	(26.9)	(15.0)	(12.3)	(15.0)	(14.1)
Chinese	54,572	222,655	730,133	1,579,866	2,089,400
	(56.2)	(71.4)	(77.6)	(76.2)	(77.7)
Indians	11,501	27,990	68,978	145,169	191,000
	(11.8)	(9.0)	(7.3)	(7.0)	(7.1)
Others	4,890	14,388	25,978	38,093	29,200
	(5.1)	(4.6)	(2.8)	(1.8)	(1.1)

Source: Department of Statistics

that the immigrant Chinese would come to outnumber the indigenous Malays, thereby turning the latter into a minority in their *Tanah Melayu*. The Malay hostility to the idea was so extreme that even after the Second World War, when the British launched the Malayan Union in 1946 and two years later the Federation of Malaya in its place, Singapore was left out of these schemes of constitutional restructuring and was maintained as a Crown Colony until the end of British rule in 1963.

Throughout, Singapore remained a multi-racial society *par excellence*. Its diverse population represented an extreme variety of races, religions, languages and cultures. During the entire period of British rule, these different peoples had largely remained separated from each other, retaining their own distinctive languages, religious beliefs and rituals, and ways of life and values. The different racial groups had their own preferred areas of habitation. The Malays were concentrated in Geylang Serai and the Indians in Anson and Serangoon. Similarly, amongst the Chinese, the Hainanese were to be found predominantly in Bras Basah, the Cantonese in Kreta Ayer, the Teochews in Havelock and the Hokkiens in Tiong Bahru. The communities had their own schools teaching through the media of their different languages and even had their own specialised economic pursuits. They essentially lived apart in their own separate worlds with little intermingling. Neither did they have the inclination nor the opportunity to get to know and develop an understanding of each other. Singapore was a plural society, representing the classical form as found by J S Furnivall before the Second World War in Burma and Java, and described by him in the following widely-quoted passage:

> In Burma as in Java, probably the first thing that strikes the visitors is the medley of people — European, Chinese, Indian and native. It is in the strictest sense a medley, for they mix but do not combine. Each group holds by its own religion, its own culture and language, its own ideas and ways. As individuals they meet, but only in the marketplace, in buying and selling. There is a plural society, with different sections of the community living side by side but separately, within the same political unit. Even in the economic sphere there is a division of labour along racial lines.[1]

To compound Singapore's diversity, each major racial group was itself fragmented on the basis of language, dialect, religion, clan or caste, and region of origin in China or in India. The Singaporean Chinese represented almost the full variety of the different regional and dialect groups from within China. They were also sharply divided on the basis of the language they spoke, as English-speaking and Chinese-speaking (mostly dialects). The Indians, though they were predominantly Tamil-speaking, included members of almost all other Indian speech communities and represented further acute internal diversity based upon religion and caste. Similarly, the indigenous Malays, despite their common religion and race, did not constitute an entirely homogenous and strongly unified group. Their fragmentation was largely based upon the Malay states of their origin in Malaya to whose sultans many among them still owed their loyalty.

The most critical demographic fact about Singapore has been that the Chinese, accounting for some 77 per cent of the population, have constituted the dominant majority. This has given the island the unique character of an essentially Chinese city state, with an overwhelming preponderance of Chinese people, capital, enterprise and industry. Much of the economic expansion and growth in the country, since separation and independence in 1965, has resulted from the special entrepreneurship, business acumen, management skills and the ability to absorb new ideas and technology of the Chinese.

Table 2: *Religious Affiliations, 1980 and 1990*

(in per cent)

Religion	1980	1990
Chinese		
Christianity	10.7	14.1
Buddhism/Taoism	72.6	68.0
Other religions	0.4	0.3
No religion	16.3	17.6
Malays		
Islam	99.6	99.7
Other religions	0.3	0.2
No religion	0.1	0.1
Indians		
Christianity	12.5	12.8
Islam	21.8	26.3
Hinduism	56.5	53.2
Other religions	8.2	6.9
No religion	1.0	0.8

Source: Department of Statistics

It is only natural for the Chinese then to view Singapore more and more as being *their* country and to want to assert themselves as the dominant majority. Inevitably, in the long run, Singapore's Chineseness is bound to show itself more and more. The important issue as such is not the predominance of the Chinese and the increasing Chineseness of Singapore, but whether in governing Singapore, that dominant majority continues to maintain a strict commitment to the founding principle of a multi-racial cultural democracy and treats its compatriots, the Malays and the Indians, as communities of equal worth.

Table 3: Predominant Household Language by Racial Group, 1980 and 1990

(in per cent)

Language	1980	1990
Chinese Households		
English	10.2	20.6
Mandarin	13.1	32.8
Chinese dialects	76.2	46.2
Others	0.5	0.4
Malay Households		
English	2.3	5.5
Malay	96.7	94.3
Others	1.0	0.2
Indian Households		
English	24.3	34.8
Malay	8.6	13.5
Tamil	52.2	43.7
Others	14.9	8.0

Source: Department of Statistics

The problem is that both the Malays and the Indians seem to be uncompromisingly committed to maintaining the ethnic deal of the 1960s, represented by the founding principle of a multiracial cultural democracy, as it was presented to them by the People's Action Party (PAP) rulers at the time. Being small minorities and lacking any significant economic and political power, they have tended to be excessively suspicious of any adaptation of the founding principle. Their concern has chiefly been with their own positions and roles, and their languages and cultures, especially in relation to the Chinese majority. They are especially sensitive to signs of any excessive ascendancy of Chinese identity, language and culture, resulting inevitably, as they view it, in a relegated status for their own languages and cultures. Behind this all is the ultimate fear that Singapore will be turned into an essentially Chinese Singapore, a Third China.

At the time of independence, based on the excessively threatening ethnic and geo-political environment in the region,

Singapore's dominant Chinese majority had little choice but to show special reasonableness towards the minorities, especially the indigenous Malays. The Chinese majority had then agreed to let the symbols of the new sovereign state of Singapore be based almost entirely upon the indigenous Malays. They had also accepted four official languages — English, Malay, Mandarin and Tamil — with Malay enjoying the special status of national language. Beyond that, they had allowed the PAP rulers, without showing any extreme hostility to the idea, to de-emphasise the Chineseness of Singapore. In all, at the time, the balance between the aspirations and interests of the Chinese and the non-Chinese had clearly been tilted in favour of the latter. Obviously, that could not be expected to last forever. Eventually a redressing of the balance, giving the Chinese majority "a fair deal", was inevitable; from the beginning, this should have been anticipated by the Malays and the Indians, and the sooner they are able to take a practical view of it and come to terms with it, the better it will be for all in Singapore.

Unfortunately, however, the especially fair and favourable treatment given to the Malay and Indian communities by the Chinese majority following independence in 1965, has generally tended to keep alive among the Malay and Indian communities unrealistically high expectations with regard to their own role and status in Singapore. It has also allowed them to continue to live with excessively strong sensitivities and continual suspicion about any manifestations of Chineseness, which are seen by them often too easily as necessarily turning the multi-racial and multi-cultural Singapore by its PAP founding fathers into a Chinese Singapore.

In this, the PAP rulers have faced a critical problem with regard to their management of Singapore's extreme ethnic diversity, especially since 1979 when they initiated their programme of Asianising Singapore. How to reconcile the growing voices within the Chinese community for special recognition of the Chinese as the dominant majority and the chief creator of the island state's spectacular economic progress and prosperity, and the insistent view of the non-Chinese minorities that it is inherent to the founding principle of cultural democracy that all ethnic groups in Singapore enjoy equal rights, role and status? How to ensure that the non-Chinese do not view the inevitably increasing Chineseness of Singapore as meaning that Singapore was eschewing the path of a multi-racial cultural democracy and was inevitably moving in the direction of a Chinese Singapore?

Note
1   J S Furnivall, *Colonial Policy and Practice*, Cambridge 1948, p. 3.

CHAPTER 2

Singapore in Malaysia: 1963–65

In the early 1960s, when Singapore was fast progressing towards decolonisation, one factor that was to influence its future the most was the critical demographic fact that the Chinese, accounting for some 77 per cent of the population, constituted the dominant majority. This had given the island a unique character of an essentially Chinese city state, with an overwhelming preponderance of Chinese people, capital, business and industry. As such, and based upon the then widespread anti-Chinese feelings among the Malay peoples in the two large countries surrounding Singapore, it was recognised by almost all Singaporeans that the island covering an area only of some 640 square kilometers could not easily establish itself as a sovereign-independent entity, and function and survive in the centre of the Malay world of Southeast Asia. They were fearful that an independent Singapore would be seen as a Chinese city state living off the wealth and raw produce of its neighbours.

The problem faced by the first-generation PAP rulers of Singapore was made even more difficult by the fact that a large majority of the Singaporean Chinese were Chinese-educated and often only spoke their Chinese dialects. They were far more Chinese in terms of their attitudes, culture and way of life than the predominantly English-educated Chinese of today's Singapore. Furthermore, Chinese chauvinism, emphasising the special distinctiveness and greatness of their language, culture, education and way of life, enjoyed considerable influence over the views and attitudes of a large majority of the Chinese. Although at that time chauvinism had strongly influenced the attitudes of all ethnic components, the chauvinism that sought to emphasise the Chineseness of Singapore posed a far more extreme threat to the future of Singapore.

It was also feared that in an independent Singapore, Chinese chauvinism, being that of the dominant majority, would be extremely difficult to curb and control. It was likely to assert itself with greater vehemence and seek to impose its will with regard to the character and bases of the country's constitution and polity, and the role and status of ethnic minorities, including the indigenous Malays. In terms of the nature of the Chinese community during the 1950s and the excessive hold of chauvinist leaders and organisations over it, it was then not easily conceivable that an independent Singapore would not be turned into a Third China.

It was the case therefore, in the late 1950s when the process of decolonisation was initiated by the British, that few in Singapore with an appreciation of the geo-political and economic realities of the region could seriously contemplate a separate, independent Singapore. The People's Action Party, which by this time had come to assume limited power under the newly introduced internal self-government arrangement, too, like almost all other political organisations, viewed the island's future only as a part of the newly independent Federation of Malaya. The PAP had "irrevocably" committed itself to the merger right from its inception in 1954. Having assumed the responsibilities of power in Singapore in 1959, Prime Minister Lee Kuan Yew and his non-communist colleagues had come to appreciate more fully the economic imperative for merger. They also had come to fear more, accentuated by their own experience of Chinese chauvinists and communists within the PAP, that the latter were likely to gain such ascendancy in an independent Singapore as to become a virtually uncontrollable force, thereby inevitably causing the political and economic destruction of the island.

Thus, during the early years of the transition to decolonisation in the late 1950s, a merger with Malaya was viewed by the first-generation PAP leaders as the only solution to the immense problems of state-making and management of ethnicity facing them as the new rulers of Singapore. They were certain that the extent of the island's ethnic diversity and the absence of any real intermingling among its diverse peoples during the period of British rule would make it virtually impossible to create a new Singapore nationhood and a polity to which all Singaporeans owed their first loyalty. Of course, they were also mindful of the fact that being western-educated and excessively westernised they themselves did not enjoy any special appeal among the common masses of the Chinese. The only way they could compete successfully against the pro-communist Chinese chauvinists, who possessed that appeal in plenty, to create a multi-racial, Singaporean Singapore, was through merger with Malaya. Their calculation was that in an essentially Malay-dominated and Malay-ruled Malaysia, those Chinese-educated who during the transition to decolonisation had increasingly begun to see themselves as the dominant majority in Singapore were more likely to — based on their status as a small minority in the enlarged federation — be willing to take a practical view of their role, shun their desire to turn the island into a Chinese Singapore and be supportive of multi-racial political organisations and politics.

In depending on merger with Malaya to ensure that ethnic contradictions did not jeopardise the future of Singapore, Prime Minister Lee Kuan Yew and his colleagues had gone against the wishes of the Chinese-educated who constituted a significant majority of the Chinese community. For tactical reasons, the Chinese-educated and their leaders had initially chosen not to oppose the merger openly, but at the same time they had used all possible covert means to frustrate the efforts of its promoters. It was obvious that most of the Chinese-educated viewed the merger as entirely inimical to their interests, for it was to deny them, constituting a large part of the dominant Chinese community, the long-awaited opportunity to rule independent Singapore.

In vindication of their view, some of the descendants of those Chinese-educated today point to the massive decline suffered by the non-Malays, especially the Chinese, in their role, status and power in Malaysia during the past three decades and the imposition of serious restrictions on their religions and cultures, and the use of their languages. They believe that if Singapore had remained a part of Malaysia, its non-Malay ethnic segments would inevitably have suffered the same fate.

The PAP rulers showed little concern that in taking the fateful decision to seek the merger of Singapore with Malaya, they had gone against the wishes of a large part of the Chinese community. Barisan Sosialis was its only feared political adversary, representing the views of Chinese chauvinists and communists, and enjoying their overwhelming support. It was largely the preponderance of the Chinese-educated, with their strong chauvinistic views and expectations, and the threat they posed to the survival of Singapore, that had moved the PAP rulers to seek to secure its future through merger with Malaya. The Chinese-educated and their leaders had no illusions about the merger plan. They were not taken in by the PAP's economic nor the other nationalistic arguments. They considered the idea as nothing more than an attempt by Singapore's small English-educated Chinese minority to maintain its privileged position and its hold on influence and power, and to deny the Chinese-educated their rightful role as the new rulers of Singapore based on their numbers.

The Chinese-educated and their leaders have, since decolonisation, felt unhappy that their views and aspirations with regard to the future of Singapore had been mostly ignored during the early 1960s when the fateful decision to merge it with Malaya was taken and again, later following separation in the mid-1960s, when the first-generation PAP rulers devised the strategy for state-making and management of ethnicity for an independent Singapore. During the past few years, with the disappearance of the communist influence among them and their full integration within the PAP, the Chinese-educated have felt less inhibited in venting their frustrations more openly and forthrightly. They have expressed their own views with regard to the nature of Singapore's multi-racialism, and the government's strategy for state-making and management of ethnicity in Singapore. The Chinese-educated are devoted to emphasising the Chineseness of the Chinese and ensuring that the evolution of the PAP government's strategy for the management of diversity for the future is geared to enhancing the identity, culture, language and traditional values of the Chinese.

It was certainly a matter of great relief for Prime Minister Lee Kuan Yew and his non-communist colleagues in the PAP, in view of the traditional Malay hostility to the idea of joining Singapore with Malaya, when in a speech to the Foreign Correspondents' Association in Singapore in May 1961, Malaysian Prime Minister Tunku Abdul Rahman surprisingly suggested that sooner or later Malaya, Singapore and the British possessions on the island of Borneo would have to work together. Fortunately for Singapore, despite considerable controversy and contentious negotiations over the next two years, the enlarged Federation of Malaysia, comprising Malaya, Singapore and the Borneo Territories, was launched on 16 September 1963.

Unfortunately, Singapore's membership of the new federation proved to be entirely unworkable. The chief reason for the confrontation and conflict between the PAP rulers of Singapore and the federal government in Kuala Lumpur, controlled by the United Malays National Organisation of the Malays, was the opposing and entirely irreconcilable views of the two with regard to the very nature of the new federation and its approach to state-making and ethnicity. Prime Minister Lee Kuan Yew and his PAP colleagues were totally uncompromising in terms of their deeply held political convictions. They believed that Malaysia, which included the indigenous Malays and a variety of minority immigrant peoples had no choice but to be a multi-racial Malaysia, a "Malaysian Malaysia", where in the words of Lee Kuan Yew, "all its peoples, irrespective of their racial origins, enjoyed the good things of life on an equal basis". To secure and enhance ethnic harmony and multi-racialism, they had offered to work together with the Malay-controlled federal government almost from the beginning and had even sought to join the "multi-racial" grouping, the Alliance, that ruled Malaysia.

But the leaders of the indigenous Malays who controlled and ruled the federal government had their own special concept of "state-making", even though in their public utterances they too sought to pay homage to the notion of a multi-racial Malaysia. To lend credibility to their persistent claims to multi-racialism, they had even accepted a constitution for the enlarged federation, almost totally based upon the 1957 Constitution of Malaya. This constitution did not recognise and entrench formally Malay political paramountcy, but instead established, clearly in principle, a multi-racial polity based upon equality of political rights for all Malaysian citizens irrespective of their racial origins (including in principle, but not in practice, the system of one person, one vote, with equal value). The political reality, however, of the Federation of Malaya as well as that of the enlarged new Federation of Malaysia that took its place was sharply different from the constitutional provisions and principles.

The general environment of ethnic goodwill and trust that had marked the period of Malayan independence in the mid-1950s, which had largely been responsible for the willing acceptance of the multi-racial constitution of 1957 by the Malays and their leaders, did not last long after independence. The deep-seated distrust and fear of the more enterprising Chinese resurfaced among the indigenous Malays, now with much enhanced intensity as their traditional protectors, the British, on whom they had relied throughout the period of British rule, had departed. With independence, the Malays and their leaders had woken up to the fact that by accepting a multi-racial polity established by the 1957 constitution, they, firstly, had failed to accord their own ethnic segment full recognition as the only *bumiputra* with the inherent right to political paramountcy. Secondly, they had obviously unleashed the obvious opportunity for the Chinese to attempt to take over their *Tanah Melayu* through their immense economic power and wealth, and the open political system based on representative democracy and fair political representation for all.

As a result, immediately following independence in 1957, the Malay political rulers of Malaya (including the charismatic and essentially non-communal Prime Minister Tunku Abdul Rahman) believed that a strategy for state-making based upon genuine multi-racialism and full political accommodation among the various ethnic segments as communities of equal worth was strongly inimical to the interests of the Malays. It was to allow the

Chinese a powerful role and in all likelihood encouraged them to seek to establish their hegemony over Malaya. They, therefore, decided to go beyond the principle of multi-racialism that constituted the foundation of the 1957 Malayan Constitution and establish a polity, through political means and without changing the constitution, that was based upon Malay control over politics, government and administration.

This dramatic departure from the inherent spirit and central feature of the 1957 constitution was, however, presented as being geared only to creating a temporary, transitional ethnic balance, a sort of *quid pro quo*, through a demarcation and separation of roles, influence and power between the indigenous Malays and the Chinese. In its operational form, it meant that the Malays would enjoy full control over politics, government and administration, and the Chinese, as well as the other immigrants, would continue to retain their special, dominant role in the economy.

Almost immediately after the new federation had come into being, this approach to state-making of the Malay political rulers, pursued with even greater vigour following the formation of Malaysia, came into direct collision with the equally strongly held commitment of Singapore's PAP leaders to the notion of a multi-racial Malaysian Malaysia. During the short period of two years that Singapore had remained part of Malaysia, it stirred up a great deal of ethnic controversy, even disharmony, through manifestation of excessive extremism among both the Malays and the Chinese. It did not take long before the federal government of Malaysia and the government of Singapore were in open confrontation and conflict. The virulence of the rhetoric and the open hostility of the Malay-controlled federal government, as well as of the Malay *raayat* at large, towards the Singaporean government would eventually result in the forced separation of Singapore.

However, the Malaysian experience was not without its positive aspects for Singapore despite the running political battles between its PAP rulers and the Malay-controlled government in Kuala Lumpur and the consequential heightening of ethnic tensions and extremism, including the 1964 communal riots in Singapore. Singaporeans and their PAP rulers had learnt a great deal that significantly influenced their attitudes towards ethnic contradictions in their own midst and gave them a fuller appreciation of Singapore's vulnerable position within the Malay world of Southeast Asia. After separation, when the PAP rulers were forced to devise their strategy hurriedly for the management of ethnicity for an independent Singapore, the experience proved to be of considerable assistance.

Firstly, Prime Minister Lee Kuan Yew and his non-communist colleagues in the Singapore government found it to their considerable advantage that they themselves did not have to deal with the threat posed by Chinese chauvinists and communists, who enjoyed strong support with the rank and file of the Chinese community. Under the Malaysia Agreement and Constitution, internal security was a responsibility of the federal government and that being the case, the problem was dealt with by the Minister of Internal Security and his department based in Kuala Lumpur. For example, the 1964 bill introducing a certificate of suitability for admission to universities, was introduced into the Malaysian parliament by the Minister of Internal Security and taken through the various stages of law-making. This bill was based upon the Singapore government's need to keep communists and chauvinists out of its two universities.

The result was that much of the repressive action against Chinese chauvinists and communists, who enjoyed widespread popularity and support among the Singaporean Chinese, was ordered and instituted by the federal government in Kuala Lumpur and its agencies in the island. Consequently, the PAP government in Singapore was largely saved the costly political awkwardness of having to inflict repression on its own Chinese people. This made it easier for the PAP rulers after separation and independence, when they had to fend for themselves and fight a critical battle against the Barisan Sosialis, representing the Chinese chauvinists and communists, for the hearts and minds of the Singaporean Chinese. Some believe that if the PAP rulers, right from the beginning in 1963, had to face and deal directly with the threat from the Chinese chauvinists and communists, they possibly would not have succeeded to the degree that they did in destroying these disruptive and damaging forces within a short period after separation from Malaysia.

Secondly, the way the PAP rulers had been able to stand up to Singaporean Malays and succeed in moderating their excessively heightened expectations and demands during this two-year period, when Singapore was a part of the essentially Malay-ruled Malaysia, proved to be immensely useful in their establishing a workable relationship with the Singaporean Malays in the post-separation, independent Singapore.

During the early 1960s, with the new Federation of Malaysia in the offing, the Singaporean Malays had begun to view themselves as a part of the larger Malaysian Malay ruling group rather than as a small, powerless ethnic minority of Singapore. It was natural for them to hope that Singapore's merger with Malaya would inevitably bring them the same special position that was enjoyed by the Malays across the causeway under the Malayan Constitution of 1957, in fact even during the preceding period of British rule. This included preferential treatment in public service employment and promotions, and quotas in respect of business licenses and entry into institutions of tertiary education. But the PAP government was entirely unwilling to compromise its overall commitment to a merit system in Singapore by giving in to Malay expectations and demands. At the time of merger, and later as a part of Malaysia, it was willing to recognise the Singaporean Malays as the *bumiputra* and accord them special treatment. But this was largely symbolic and not of much benefit to the Malays in real terms. For example, the PAP government in Singapore designated Malay as the national language and undertook to safeguard Malay political, economic, religious and cultural interests. It offered the Malays special financial support to enable them to take advantage of educational opportunities, but not any preferential treatment and quotas.

In the post-separation Singapore, this experience had a definite containing effect on Malay expectations and demands. It even had a lasting influence on their view of PAP rulers and government. The community realised that it had to deal with a group of leaders who were tough and could not be "kicked around". They could not be pushed into compromising their fundamental commitments for the sake of political expediency. Even during the period when Malaysia was ruled by their compatriots across the causeway, the Singaporean Malays had only been able to push the PAP leaders into according them a purely symbolic, special status as the *bumiputra*. After independence, the community has tended to take a pragmatic view of its importance as the *bumiputra* and its ability to extract concessions from the government.

Thirdly, it gave Singapore's PAP rulers as well as its citizenry, especially the Chinese, an experience of how easily intense emotions could be stirred up and be exploited by irresponsible politicians and political organisations. The turbulent relationship with the Malay leadership of the federal government in Kuala Lumpur served as a clear warning that Singapore could ignore its geo-political and ethnic compulsions only at its peril. This made it much easier for Prime Minister Lee Kuan Yew and his colleagues, after independence, to base their strategy for the management of ethnicity on rational and practical considerations. More importantly, they were able to get it accepted by most of the Chinese of Singapore. But for the sobering influence of the two years as a part of Malaysia, the PAP rulers would have found it greatly more difficult to deal with and curb the expectations of many Singaporean Chinese to have an essentially Chinese Singapore and get them to agree to a multi-racial Singaporean Singapore.

Unfortunately, Singapore did not last long in the new federation because of the deep-seated, general distrust and fear of the Chinese among the indigenous Malays, especially their political rulers in Malaya. Within two years of merger, in mid-1965, Singapore was virtually forced to leave Malaysia. It was a shattering blow to the PAP leaders who had throughout been deeply dedicated to building Singapore into a model multi-racial and multi-cultural city state within Malaysia rather than letting it be turned into a Third China. With separation went the very foundation of their entire approach to the problems of ethnicity and state-building — merger with Malaya. Singapore's PAP rulers were forced to reconsider and redesign their strategy for state-making and management of ethnicity in the new context of an independent Singapore.

CHAPTER 3

Cultural Democracy: The Founding Principle

In mid-1965, after a short and extremely turbulent two-year existence as a member of the Federation of Malaysia, Singapore was separated. This represented a cruel twist of fate for Singaporeans as during the transition to decolonisation only a few years before, they — excepting their Chinese-educated compatriots considered by them as entirely misguided — had fully subscribed to the view that the future of their miniscule island was irrevocably tied with Malaya. They did not contemplate an independent Singapore as an even remotely viable and realistic proposition. Now, with separation forced upon them, the pro-merger Singaporeans had been left with no choice but to accept independence and deal with the problems of setting up a new, separate, sovereign Republic of Singapore.

The first-generation PAP rulers hurriedly had to devise an approach to management of ethnic diversity that was suited to Singapore's new status as a sovereign independent republic, but at the same time ensured that Singapore was not viewed as a Third China. Fortunately for them, they did not have to start from scratch as happened in British colonial possessions elsewhere. Before decolonisation during the mid-1950s, the British, faced with a deepening sense of alienation among the Chinese and an increasingly threatening manifestation of Chinese chauvinism and communism, had uncharacteristically sought to deal with the special problems of state-building in Singapore.

In 1955, an All Party Committee on Chinese Education was set up. It produced an impressive report in 1956 that contained far-reaching recommendations. The important recommendations of the committee were:

1. Recognition of Malay as the national language.
2. Recognition of Malay, English, Chinese and Tamil as the official languages.
3. Official acceptance of Chinese-medium, Malay-medium and Tamil-medium schools for purposes of government funding and recognition of the certificates of schools that followed a new national curriculum.
4. Compulsory bi-lingualism in primary education and tri-lingualism in secondary education.
5. Introduction of new national textbooks that especially promoted among students a sense of identification with Singapore, in all schools irrespective of their medium of instruction.
6. Use of extracurricular activities in schools to especially promote inter-ethnic understanding and contact.[1]

The recommendations, based upon the overall objective of promoting ethnic integration, sought to foster a Singaporean identity among all the diverse peoples of the island and facilitate inter-ethnic contact and understanding.

Almost all the major recommendations of the committee were implemented soon afterwards, in 1959, by the first popularly-based PAP government which had assumed power under the newly introduced system of limited self-government. The new PAP government was obviously happy to introduce the chief recommendations of the committee because these had fully reflected their own approach to the issue and their integrative agenda for Singapore.

Later, between 1963 and 1965, Singapore's membership of the new Federation of Malaysia had not necessitated any significant change in the PAP government's approach to Singapore's ethnic diversity and their own integrative agenda. However, in 1965, following separation and independence, their approach and agenda had to be carefully adapted to the new situation in which they alone took the decisions and held responsibility for the future well-being of Singapore. They also had to work out the details of the overall approach, taking into account the new ethnic and political compulsions. It was a formidable challenge for Prime Minister Lee Kuan Yew and his colleagues because the future survival and progress of Singapore depended on their success. They knew that any extreme manifestations of ethnic disharmony and conflict could easily destroy the new republic in its infancy.

The problem had been made even more acute for the leaders of the Singapore government because during the two years 1963–65, when Singapore was a part of Malaysia, Indonesian "confrontation" and the excessive acrimony between them and the Malay leaders of the federal government in Kuala Lumpur had a damaging effect on the ethnic environment and relationships in Singapore as well as within the region. In Singapore, they had to deal with their own different ethnic groups on issues of vital concern whose attitudes towards each other were now guided more by fear and distrust than by understanding and mutual respect. Heightened ethnic sensitivities and emotions had taken hold of many Singaporeans — Malay, Chinese and Indian — and, as a result, it was not easy to expect them to be capable of considering the critical ethnic issues facing their state with rationality and good sense. Furthermore, the special external constraints, which then impinged excessively on the PAP government's choice of policies, were of such a sensitive nature that they could not at all be discussed and debated publicly. The PAP rulers therefore could not afford to follow the normal democratic practice of seeking out a national consensus on the critical issues of state-building through a full and unfettered public debate. The result was that the PAP's approach to management of ethnicity was devised during the mid-1960s without any real consultation with and involvement of the people of Singapore.

Externally, the relationship of the PAP rulers of Singapore with their closest neighbours Indonesia and Malaysia could not have been any more strained. Even though the coup of September 1965 had changed the Indonesian political situation dramatically, the legacy of Indonesian "confrontation" had continued to cast its dark shadow. It was to be many years before Singapore and Indonesia were able to develop mutual trust and a workable relationship between themselves. In Malaysia, there were powerful, popular Malay leaders in the government as well as outside who were extremely angry that Prime Minister Tunku Abdul Rahman by pre-emptively forcing Singapore to separate, had denied them the opportunity to deal with the territory and its PAP leaders more severely, such as detaining some of them and imposing federal control over Singapore. They were not willing to let the small island territory, which to them was an integral part of their *Tanah Melayu*, be separated from Malaya that easily and be "handed over" entirely to the Chinese.

There was acute fear among Singaporeans and their leaders of their large and powerful Malay neighbours, whom they felt could not easily be relied upon to always act rationally. Singapore thus felt strongly threatened. The PAP rulers knew that their policies and behaviour, especially on ethnic issues, were being watched closely. As a result, they had to be careful to ensure that these were of a nature that could not be misconstrued. It is important to keep in mind that for Prime Minister Lee Kuan Yew and his colleagues during those formative years of independence, sheer survival of Singapore was the overriding imperative. They could not afford to pursue policies or take state action relating both to domestic issues and to their international relationships which were likely to incur the wrath of their neighbours. They had to take into account the special sensitivities of their Malay neighbours and not always insist upon asserting their sovereign right as an independent state to pursue policies dictated by their own national interests.

On the whole, for the PAP rulers the external and the internal political and ethnic environment of the mid-1960s were not the most congenial for designing their approach to management of ethnicity. However, their task had been made somewhat easier, at least in one important respect. An overwhelming majority of Singaporeans were immigrants who had been treated mostly as transient aliens, enjoying few citizenship rights during British rule. Not many among them had then viewed Singapore as home. They did not have the same emotional attachment and sense of belonging to Singapore as the Singaporean Malays then and an increasing number of Singaporean Chinese today. As a result, most immigrant non-Malays had not articulated any clear and considered ideas and expectations of their own with regard to the broad framework of ethnic relationships in an independent Singapore. Their concerns had related largely to the issue of their distinctive identities, languages and cultures. Only the Chinese-educated Chinese among them seemed to have their own special views on these vital issues. But as they were widely viewed as a disruptive and dangerous chauvinist-communist group, the PAP rulers did not have to show any special inclination to consider their views nor to seek their consent. Later, in the late 1980s, it was only when the Chinese-educated had been able to shed their communist connections that they were able to raise these issues publicly and present their own special perspective on them. A senior leader of the present PAP government told this writer recently:

> The Chinese-speaking, who had then viewed themselves as a part of the larger Chinese world and had espoused strongly the cause of Chinese communism and chauvinism, had thereby disabled themselves from being consulted with regard to the government's strategy for the management of ethnicity. And this, ever since, had made it difficult for the Chinese-speaking to fully commit themselves to the strategy.[2]

Thus, in devising their approach to the management of ethnicity, the PAP rulers did not have any special worries about ensuring from the beginning that their own ideas enjoyed the willing consent of Singaporeans. As we noted above, the Chinese-educated had largely disabled themselves from having any influence and role in this regard. As for the remaining non-Malays, mostly the Indians and the English-educated Chinese, the PAP rulers saw no special problems because their founding principle of a multi-racial cultural democracy was in harmony with the broad expectations of these groups. Constituting only a small minority, the Indians, on the whole, had a realistic view of their position and did not expect a great deal. Essentially what they sought was a multi-racial Singapore that did not allow any discrimination against them and ensured that they were able to secure their own place in the sun. In any case, during those days most Indians were staunch PAP supporters and many of them tended to view it as their party. Similarly, there was no problem with regard to the English-educated Chinese as they formed the chief supporters and promoters of the PAP. They had provided most of its leaders and as such they constituted much of the new ruling class of Singapore.

Of all the ethnic segments in Singapore, the PAP rulers had to worry immediately only about the indigenous Malays. They had to take into account their views on ethnic issues and ensure that the government's view of their status as the *bumiputra* and its approach to and management of ethnicity were not entirely unacceptable to the Malays. During the preceding period when Singapore was a part of Malaysia, the Malays had possibly been the most unhappy group of all because the PAP government of Singapore had refused to accord them a special position beyond the purely symbolic. As Singapore was a part of Malaysia, it had been a natural expectation of the Malays that their status in Singapore and their treatment by the state government would follow the provisions of the Malayan Constitution of 1957 and that they would be accorded a special position similar to that enjoyed by their Malay compatriots in the rest of Malaysia. In order to pressure the PAP government on the issue of the Malay special position, in July 1964 the Singapore United Malays National Organisation (a part of the Malaysian ruling party, United Malays National Organisation, UMNO) had organised a Malay Convention which was attended by representatives of some 150 Malay cultural, religious and educational organisations. Before the convention, the Singapore UMNO published a position paper entitled "The Situation of Malays in Singapore" in which were included the following demands to the PAP government on behalf of the Malay community:

1. Further Malay settlements and land reservations.
2. Lower public housing rents for Malays.
3. Promotion of the Malay language in government departments and business firms.

4. Free transportation, schoolbooks and tuition for Malay students.
5. More scholarships for Malays at every educational level.
6. Legislation to guarantee Malay employment (by which Singapore UMNO meant job quotas, special business licenses and the kind of privileges extended to Malays in Malaysia under the *bumiputra* policies).[3]

The Malays in Singapore had been especially unhappy because the Malays in Sarawak and Sabah, the states that had remained separated from Malaya like Singapore, with the Malays constituting only a small minority, had secured a better deal than what had been offered to them. As a result, the PAP rulers, during that two-year period, had to make strenuous, but not entirely successful, efforts to talk with the representatives and leaders of the Singaporean Malays in order to pacify them and contain their growing alienation and anger based on the critical issue of their status in Singapore as the *bumiputra*.

After separation, the Malays in Singapore could not openly look up to the Malay-controlled government in Kuala Lumpur for support any longer. The PAP rulers, however, had no choice but to continue to deal with them with special care because many Malay leaders in Malaysia, including those in the government as well as outside, had continued to see themselves and present themselves as the protectors of their kith and kin in Singapore. In Singapore, certainly for some years, separation from Malaysia had not altered things a great deal to most Malays and their leaders. They still saw themselves as an integral part of the larger *Tanah Melayu* Malay community and derived a certain sense of powerfulness from it. Their expectations with regard to their role and status and their treatment by the Singapore government during the early years of Singapore independence were based upon this sense of powerfulness. Thus the PAP rulers had to ensure that their own ideas and policies with regard to management of ethnicity were, on the whole, not entirely unacceptable to the Singaporean Malays.

In terms of their own strongly held personal values and convictions, and their view of what was necessary to ensure Singapore's survival, progress and prosperity, Prime Minister Lee

Kuan Yew and his close associates had no choice but to continue with their ideal of cultural democracy, representing multi-racialism, multi-culturalism and multi-lingualism, as the paramount founding principle of independent Singapore. This was the concept, reflected in the slogan of a Malaysian Malaysia, for which they had battled while in Malaysia and which eventually had brought about Singapore's forced separation from the federation.

The PAP rulers had developed this approach to management of ethnicity in 1959, during the period of British rule, when they had been first voted to power in Singapore. However, it is important to note that their view during that pre-Malaysia period differed in one important aspect from the one they were to articulate later in the mid-1960s, after Singapore had been separated from Malaysia. Before Malaysia, their view of a multi-racial cultural democracy included their commitment to creating a national Malayan culture as a vital element. In terms of their strongly held view that Singapore could neither survive nor prosper without merging itself with the Malay-ruled Malaya, their concept of a national Malayan culture accorded a special place to the Malays, as the *bumiputra*, and their language and culture. They had already recognised Malay as the national language of Singapore and it was obvious that they had no problems in accepting and promoting a national Malayan culture that was substantially based upon the heritage of the indigenous Malays. Clearly, their real concern was that in an enlarged Malaya, which included Singapore, the cultures and languages of the Chinese and Indians were not suppressed in the name of creating a national culture and that they were recognised as constituting a vital part of the national Malayan culture.

However, separation from Malaysia and independence in 1965 had dramatically changed the context. If the PAP rulers were to continue with their commitment to promoting a common national culture, they now had to think in terms of a national *Singaporean* culture. Because of the fact that the Chinese accounted for more than three-quarters of the population of Singapore, it was no more possible to promote the idea of a national culture that was substantially based on the heritage of the indigenous Malays. Undoubtedly, the Malays had remained recognised in independent Singapore as the *bumiputra*, but now they represented only a small minority, accounting for some fifteen per cent of the population.

The problem was that the PAP rulers could not, at the same time, afford to substantially base the notion of a Singaporean national culture on the Chinese, who constituted a dominant majority. The fear of their powerful Malay neighbours precluded that entirely, and, in any case, they had never considered that to be a workable notion. In view of this awkward problem after separation and independence in 1965, at first, the PAP rulers did not identify the creation of a Singaporean national culture explicitly as a special objective. Later, starting from the 1980s, when it began to be considered necessary for Singapore to preserve and enhance its extreme ethnic diversity, they began to discard it altogether from their agenda.

Besides its innate worth in terms of the values it represented, the founding principle of a multi-racial cultural democracy was critical to the management of ethnicity by the first-generation PAP rulers. Firstly, it gave the Chinese-dominated PAP government a good image as being reasonable in offering the country's small, powerless ethnic minorities, including the indigenous Malays, a fair deal. This was of critical importance to the new state of Singapore, especially in terms of its relationship with its large Malay neighbours, Malaysia and Indonesia. Secondly, internally in Singapore, it offered the indigenous Malays and the Indians an ethnic framework that they could not easily disagree with and which could encourage them to develop a sense of identification with Singapore and confidence in the ethnic credentials of the PAP government. Thirdly, as a broad-based founding principle, it had a special virtue that it did not necessarily have to be altered in the future. Political prudence required that a society as ethnically fragmented as Singapore could not afford to allow periodic public discussion and debate by future generations of its people on the highly emotion-laden issue without exposing the country to damaging ethnic controversy. Finally, from a public policy perspective, its broad-based nature was again a special asset as it made it possible for the founding principle to be adapted and reinterpreted periodically to meet the requirements of the changing ethnic and political realities of Singapore in the future.

The importance attached to the concept by the PAP's first-generation leaders was reflected in the fact that after separation, at the first session of the first Singapore parliament on 22 December 1965, the government appointed a Constitutional Commission to formulate constitutional safeguards required to protect this founding principle. The Minister of Law and National Development stated that

> . . . one of the cornerstones of the policy of the government is a multi-racial Singapore. We are a nation comprising people of various races who constitute her citizens, and our citizens are equal regardless of differences of race, language, culture and religion.
>
> Whilst a multi-racial secular society is an ideal espoused by many, it is a dire necessity for our survival in the midst of turmoil and the pressures of big power conflict in an area where new nationalisms are seeking to assert themselves in the place of the old European empires in Asia. In such a setting, a nation based on one race, one language and one religion, when its people are multi-racial, is doomed for destruction.[4]

From the beginning the PAP rulers sought to totally debunk the "ideology of a mono-cultural, mono-lingual and mono-racial people ruled by an authoritarian state", as a clear message to the Chinese-educated Singaporean.[5] They said that it was followed in certain countries where it had meant that "the rulers who represent the racial majority insist on one exclusive language and culture. This is imposed by decree on the minorities, often on pain of mass expulsions or other punitive impositions."[6] They repudiated the assimilationist approach of requiring the minorities to discard their traditional cultures and adopt the culture of the majority group, including, in some countries, attempts to make members of minority groups change even their names and surnames. Based on their own experience, during 1963–65, of the potentially assimilationist approach of the Malay-dominated Malaysian government, they were keen to establish in Singapore a multi-racial cultural democracy that could act as a model for other Southeast Asian countries, all of which had significant Chinese and other Asian minorities.

The PAP leaders viewed assimilation as an entirely destructive one-way process, in which those who refused to follow the dictates of the majority were often either expelled or otherwise penalised. They sought to warn the Singaporean Chinese, especially the Chinese-educated, of the inherent dangers in the assimilationist approach by presenting a grim historical picture of the horrendous suffering and violence inflicted by it in a variety of countries:

> The United States destroyed nearly two-thirds of the Indian population before her policy changed. The small Tasmanian population was completely wiped out by the British. The Boers of South Africa looked upon the Hottentots as scarcely more than animals of the jungle and hunted them ruthlessly. In Spain, three million Moors were expelled from the country just because they refused to give up their Moorish way of life and have their children educated by Christian priests. Germany between 1933 and 1945, murdered six million people, the majority of whom were Jews.[7]

The PAP rulers also refused entirely to subscribe to the strongly held view in newly decolonised countries, including their neighbours in the region, that in order to create and enhance national unity, cultural, educational and linguistic diversity had to be reduced, if not to be eliminated altogether. They considered cultural democracy as being the most realistic way of dealing with Singapore's ethnic realities. They were especially influenced by the success of this approach in Switzerland. The merit of the concept to them was that it regarded cultural diversity as a source of vitality for a nation and as a stimulus to cultural advancement rather than a threat to unity. It rejected the notion of cultural uniformity and upheld the ideal of equal freedom for minorities and majorities alike in language, culture, religion and way of life. It included

> . . . appreciation and respect for one another's cultural heritage, and a conscious effort by all diverse communities to fuse some of their elements into a national cultural pattern rather than complete repression of the culture of the minorities. Cultural democracy is based on equality, tolerance, justice and harmony.[8]

It is significant that this PAP view did not stipulate, as before in 1959, the necessity to create a common national culture. Instead, now after separation from Malaysia, it looked forward only to the development of "a national cultural pattern" in Singapore.

Based upon these ideas, Prime Minister Lee Kuan Yew and his colleagues established Singapore as a multi-racial cultural democracy after separation in 1965. One pre-eminent member of that group of founding fathers, S Rajaratnam, recently outlined to this writer the following as the critical components of the PAP's 'strategy to turn their founding principle into a practical reality:

1. De-emphasising the Chineseness of Singapore and getting the Chinese not to insist on securing a status and role that reflected their numerical dominance in the population (he mentioned this as the first element of their strategy based upon the foremost fear in 1965 that an independent Singapore was to be inevitably viewed by its neighbours as a Third China).
2. According the Malays a special position as the *bumiputra*.
3. Establishing a multi-racial, multi-cultural and multi-lingual Singaporean Singapore in which all ethnic groups were accorded an equal status under the constitution.
4. Ensuring a fair economic deal for all through continuing economic expansion and growth.
5. Providing an administration — including the executive, the judiciary and the public service — that reflected ethnic sensitivity, but accorded fair treatment to all, irrespective of their ethnic background.[9]

The PAP rulers established an independent Singapore that accorded recognition to all ethnic segments as communities of equal worth, as sub-nationalities, and guaranteed them equal rights with regard to their distinctive identities, cultures, religions and languages. Its polity did not distinguish between people on the basis of their ethnicity and guaranteed them equal political rights and fair political representation through an electoral system that followed the principle of one person, one vote, with equal value. The Chinese, who constituted an overwhelming majority of the population, were not accorded any constitutionally-entrenched special privileges, status or treatment. There were no provisions in the constitution that entrusted political power to the Chinese and insisted, for example, that only a Chinese could occupy the position of head of government. Central to the founding principle of a multi-racial cultural democracy was the notion that all communities, irrespective of their size and wealth, would enjoy an equal status and equal rights. The first-generation PAP rulers held such an extreme view of this critical precept that they had expected that in their multi-racial Singapore, ethnic minorities would not even retain the consciousness of being minorities. Prime Minister Lee Kuan Yew said, soon after Singapore became independent in 1965:

> The problem was how to create a situation where the minority, either in ethnic, linguistic or religious terms, was not conscious that it was a minority, and that the exercise of its rights as equal citizens with all others was so natural and so accepted by society that it was not conscious of the fact that it was sharing equal rights with the others in dominant ethnic groups.[10]

In line with their founding principle of a cultural democracy, the PAP rulers took a practical view even of the notion of loyalty to Singapore. They did not make any excessive demands on their nationals in the name of loyalty, such as calling upon them to be willing to shed or dilute their separate ethnic identities and attachments for the sake of a common national identity, culture and language. The commitment of the different ethnic segments to their own distinctive identities, cultures, heritages, languages and ways of life was not seen as detracting from their loyalty to Singapore. It is important to note that the different ethnic segments were, in effect, recognised as constituting distinctive sub-nationalities of a multi-racial Singaporean nation. They were not required to discard nor to submerge their Chineseness, Malayness or Indianness for the sake of a new Singaporean national identity. In fact, based upon that vital notion, today the PAP government views its role as not being restricted only to ensuring the survival of the different identities, languages and cultures. As we shall see later, it now actively seeks their enhancement.

Explaining his view on the vital issue of management of ethnicity Prime Minister Lee Kuan Yew, the pre-eminent founding father of modern Singapore, told this writer in 1969, a few years after independence:

> I do not believe one can legislate for integration or assimilation. It is not subject to such mandatory orders. What we can do is to create a situation in which, on the fundamental issues, those vital for the survival of the community, of the nation, there cannot be any differences or divergence of interest or opinion. Whether you are of Chinese, Indian, Malay, Eurasian or Ceylonese descent, when it comes to the survival of Singapore, you or rather we, must all be one: i.e. Singapore must be defended and her interests upheld for everyone's benefit. On that there can be no disagreement. And if Singapore's interests conflict with those of China, or India, or Indonesia, or any country, then the interests of Singapore must prevail. On this, and the values we build into our young, there can be no argument. This is being systematically inculcated in our schools: we raise the flag every morning and take a vow to defend Singapore and build a society whose fruits will be enjoyed by all of us.[11]

Mindful of the extreme slowness of the process of intermingling and its impact on diversity, he added:

> Beyond these essentials, it is best to leave it to time and circumstance to decide whether there will be ethnic assimilation or a cultural homogeneity blurring out the cultural boundaries now co-existing. My personal

observation is that ethnic assimilation is a very slow, very marginal process. It does take place. People do marry outside their own ethnic groups. I cannot help noticing that with the older civilisations, particularly the Indians with their caste system, and also the Chinese, even though they have clans which are less of a divide than caste, there is a deep sense of their distinctiveness and a desire, probably just egoism, on the part of the parents to see in their offspring a recognisable image of themselves.

My expectation is that there will always be a small group of the adventurous in all the ethnic groups, perhaps those who are less egotistical, who marry across ethnic lines. But they will probably be in the minority. Therefore the chances are that if you come back to Singapore a century from now, you would find people more or less the same.[12]

The core element of this practical approach to the management of ethnicity was that, whether one liked it or not, Singapore's ethnic diversity was there to stay. It was based on some of the oldest civilisations that constitute the proud heritage of humanity. There was not a great deal that could be achieved through state action in attempting to blur out the different identities of Singaporeans and create homogeneity. Attempts in this regard were not only bound to fail, but would also prove immensely damaging to ethnic relationships. It was better to view diversity as an asset, as culturally enriching for all Singaporeans, and to give Singapore an advantage, at least to start with, in building itself as a premier tourist destination in the region. Today's tourist brochures, taking full advantage of that diversity, successfully present Singapore as Instant Asia.

Even though the PAP rulers, in terms of their technocratic and intellectual abilities, believed that there was not much that could not be achieved through human ingenuity, management of ethnicity was one area in which they resisted their temptation to indulge themselves excessively in social engineering to overly influence and manipulate the linguistic and cultural diversity to secure "a national cultural pattern". They took the view that the proper role of the state was to create an overall environment as free as possible of contentious ethnic controversy and confrontation, in which the different peoples were able to intermix freely and savour the differences. It was important that in dealing with the emotion-laden issues involving management of ethnicity, the government established only a broad founding principle, a general overall framework, that was not in contradiction with the views and expectations of a large part of the country's ethnically diverse citizenry. A pre-eminent first-generation leader of government, S Rajaratnam, told this writer a few years ago:

> We work on the basis that there is a wide gap between the collective and individual commitments of people. Individually they tend to be more pragmatic . . .
> We satisfy their emotions by publicly having a policy which does not humiliate them, which is not totally contrary to their collective commitment. We tell them, "Yes, you can send your children to Chinese or Tamil schools and you can use Mandarin and Tamil wherever you like, including the Parliament." When you are dealing with emotions, expecially where they are right emotions, you never meet them head-on. You work your way around them. People don't keep on pushing a door that is open. We opened the door by adopting the policy that all languages and schools were equal and parents had the right to send children to the schools of their liking.[13]

A multi-racial cultural democracy represented that broad founding framework that could not easily be viewed as being contrary to the collective commitments of the different ethnic segments. The PAP rulers were certain that this was bound to satisfy the emotions of most Singaporeans and in so doing, secure their willing backing for it.

In general terms, the founding principle meant autonomy to all the various ethnic components with regard to their cultures, religions and languages. But from the beginning, the PAP rulers had made it certain that this autonomy was allowed to be used only within clearly circumscribed limits. The government's own role in relation to this autonomy was not to be an essentially non-interventionist onlooker. The first-generation PAP rulers were not willing to abdicate their overriding obligation to maintain Singapore's integrity and security, and promote the well-being of its peoples. The limitations on ethnic autonomy that they devised were based on the following: firstly, that ethnic autonomy was not misused to promote ethnic, cultural, linguistic and religious chauvinism by any group; secondly, that it did not damage inter-ethnic relationships and promote disharmony; and thirdly, that it did not jeopardise Singapore's vital political and economic interests and international relationships.

In all, the PAP rulers' concept of a multi-racial cultural democracy constituted an essentially pragmatic response to the internal ethnic imperatives as well as the regional geopolitical compulsions. Later, however, starting from the late 1980s, they were able to begin to view Singapore's ethnic diversity as a special asset that needed to be preserved and enhanced. They began to take a more positive and active view of their own role in this regard.

Prime Minister Lee Kuan Yew and his colleagues, in dealing with the problem of ethnic diversity, considered it of paramount importance to change the socio-economic environment significantly in which their citizens lived and worked. It was essential to them that Singapore achieved rapid and continuing economic expansion and progress so that Singaporeans could be provided adequate employment, housing, health, education and improved standards of living. The socio-economic environment at the time was not very different from that in the premier cities of most other underdeveloped, Third World countries.

It was a world of massive over-crowding, poverty, unemployment, illiteracy and low standards of living that bred an attitude of extreme ethnic anger, distrust and unreasonableness in which it was extremely difficult to achieve the delicate balance and harmony between conflicting demands and aspirations of the different ethnic groups that composed the population of Singapore. It was a setting of fear and prejudice that had been continually exploited by opportunistic politicians and political organisations to secure popular support based on ethnicity. Ethnic exclusiveness and solidarity added to the potential for ethnic confrontation, violence and conflict which had often threatened the existence of many Third World states during the past two decades. The PAP rulers were fully aware of the inherent problems of attempting to manage Singapore's extreme ethnic diversity in that environment. They were also certain that "to combat effectively the competing loyalties and other primordial ties exerted on the local population by their countries of origin, the citizens must be given a stake in Singapore."[14] Therefore, from the beginning, they considered economic advancement and growth to be a core element of their strategy for the management of ethnicity and they gave it the necessary priority.

Thus the PAP rulers sought to achieve maximum economic growth and prosperity, and directed much of their attention and energies to that end. They especially designed a "democracy that works", with institutions and processes of government, and even the character and functioning of their People's Action Party, whose first purpose was to facilitate continuing economic expansion and growth. They did not permit untrammelled political activity and expected Singaporeans to primarily preoccupy themselves with producing wealth and prosperity. A modernising technocratic leadership, with few political skills, was especially recruited and trained for the purpose. The result was that Singapore's economy achieved spectacular progress during the 1970s. It produced unprecedented opportunities for making money and created such a high level of satisfaction with their material existence for a significantly large part of Singapore's citizenry that few of them were willing to indulge in destructive ethnic disharmony and confrontation.

As we noted before, the founding principle of a multi-racial cultural democracy represented only a broad framework. As a result, the way the broad framework's continuing relevance and full effectiveness could always be maintained was by regularly adapting its detailed content, interpretation and emphases in operational policy with the changing reality of ethnic relationships, social and educational advancement, and economic progress and prosperity in Singapore. Externally, it was based upon the country's relations with its large Malay neighbours and the geo-political environment in the Southeast Asian region.

We shall now look at the way the founding principle of

cultural democracy was used and interpreted at different times by the first-generation PAP leaders to deal with the changing compulsions and realities that confronted them during their long tenure as the rulers of Singapore from 1965 to 1990.

Table 4: *Economic Indicators, 1972 and 1982*

	1972	1982
1. **National Income**		
GNP (million $)	8,135	30,379
Per capita GNP ($)	3,206	10,061
2. **Industrial Production**		
Establishments	1,971	3,581
Workers	175,241	274,106
Output (million $)	6,126	36,266
Value Added (million $)	1,820	9,391
3. **Construction**		
Buildings Commenced (thousand m^2)	4,276	13,622
Under Construction (thousand m^2)	7,261	25,251
Buildings Completed (thousand m^2)	3,049	5,513
4. **External Trade**		
Imports (million $)	9,538	60,244
Exports (million $)	6,149	44,244
5. **Cargo Handled**		
Seaborne (thousand tonnes)	57,064	95,660
Airborne (tonnes)	30,529	222,304
6. **Official Foreign Reserves (million $)**	4,929	17,917
7. **Central Provident Fund (million $)**	1,316	15,655
8. **Tourist Arrivals (thousands)**	783	2,965

Source: Department of Statistics

Notes

1 C S Kong, "Nation-Building in Singapore, A Historical Perspective", in Jon S T Quah (editor), *In Search of Singapore's National Values*, Institute of Policy Studies, Singapore 1990, p. 13.
2 Interview with a senior leader of the present PAP government, Singapore, 25 January 1994.
3 *Making the Difference: Ten Years of MENDAKI*, Singapore 1989, p. 36.
4 *Report of the Constitutional Commission, 1966*, Singapore 1966, p. 1.

5 K C Lee (Minister of State for Culture), *National Culture in a Multi-Racial Society*, Ministry of Culture, Singapore 1967, p. 1.
6 *Ibid.*, p. 1
7 *Ibid.*, p. 4.
8 *Ibid.*, p. 5.
9 Interview with S Rajaratnam, Singapore, November 1992.
10 Quoted in *Singapore Yearbook, 1967*, pp. 3–4.
11 Interview with Lee Kuan Yew, Singapore, 1969.
12 *Ibid.*
13 Interview with S Rajaratnam, Singapore, December 1982.
14 Jon S T Quah, "Government Policies and Nation-Building", in Jon S T Quah (editor), *In Search of Singapore's National Values*, Institute of Policy Studies, Singapore 1990, p. 46.

CHAPTER 4

Managing Ethnic Diversity: The First Phase, 1965–79

In working out the application of their broad-based founding principle of a multi-racial cultural democracy, Prime Minister Lee Kuan Yew and his first-generation colleagues first had to deal with three special compulsions that could not be ignored and required to be handled with extreme care and sensitivity.

1. *De-emphasising the Chineseness of Singapore*
The PAP rulers had to ensure that the Chinese did not insist upon securing a special role and status for themselves nor their culture and language, based upon their being the dominant majority. It was critical to the need to de-emphasise the Chineseness of Singapore. Many Chinese believed that their community as well as their culture and language were owed a special role and status in an independent Singapore ruled by Singaporeans as a matter of right. During the 1950s and 1960s, demands had been made by prominent and powerful Chinese business and community leaders to recognise Chinese as the language of the emerging nation of Singapore.

This view was derived from the demographic reality of their community accounting for so much as three-quarters of the population, clearly being the dominant majority. It was further reinforced by the fact that during the British period, the Chinese had contributed the most in turning the small island into the premier centre of trade and commerce in the Southeast Asian region. Their feelings on this issue had been especially strong, not only because during that period their contribution to the growth and prosperity of Singapore had not been given any special recognition but also because, in certain ways, they had not been accorded a political role and voice equivalent to that enjoyed by the small Indian minority. When in 1948 elections were first introduced by the British in the colony, a far greater number of Indians had been enfranchised and given the right to vote than the Chinese.[1]

In multi-ethnic societies, where a single ethnic segment constitutes a large majority, it is only natural for that group to insist that it be clearly recognised and accepted as the dominant majority, and that the language and the symbols of the state be based on those of that ethnic segment. If in 1965 independent Singapore had been constituted essentially as a Third China, it could not have been viewed as something extraordinary. Looking back, it is only fair to say that it was quite extraordinary and remarkable that independent Singapore was able to launch itself as, and maintain ever since, a genuinely multi-racial, multi-cultural and multi-lingual social and political entity.

In such states, it is also deemed usual for the relationship between the dominant majority and the others to be that of a majority-minority or dominant-subordinate. The dominance of the majority is regarded as an accepted fact, and ethnic minorities are rarely able to secure and enjoy much influence and power in their own right. They often have to live on sufferance and be willing to respect and abide by the wishes of the majority. They have to accept the state with its image, language and symbols, such as the flag and the national anthem, based mostly upon the culture and heritage of the majority. In such societies all over the world, even attempts at forced assimilation by curbing or destroying the separate identities, cultures and languages of the minorities in order to create a nation of one people, one culture and one language, are not all that uncommon and are not easily viewed as illegitimate and unfair.

Singapore's Chinese had been conscious of the treatment meted out to their kith and kin in almost all countries of the Southeast Asian region by the majority ethnic segments as a part of their policy of creating a unified nation of one people, one culture and one language. They had a collective awareness that their fellow Chinese were not only denied fair political status and rights based upon their position as citizens, but that they were also forced to accept limitations, often extreme and unreasonable, on the use of their languages and manifestations of their distinctive culture. In some countries, even the use of the Chinese family and given names was frowned upon, if not altogether denied for official purposes. Based upon that treatment of the Chinese elsewhere in the region and their own experience of powerlessness during the period of British rule, it was only natural for many Chinese, especially the Chinese-educated, to view independent Singapore as a Chinese city state where they could assume the reins of power and build its polity and its society based largely upon their own heritage, culture, aspirations and inclinations. Essentially, they believed that independence had offered them an opportunity to occupy their rightful position as the rulers of *their* country and assert its Chineseness.

The first-generation PAP rulers, who then drew only limited support from the Chinese, had been faced with the task of curbing the latter's natural urge to assert their dominance and persuade them to accept a multi-racial Singapore, a Singaporean Singapore, that did not unduly emphasise its Chineseness. They had to persuade them not to insist on behaving and acting as the dominant majority, which they undeniably were, and treating the Malays, the Indians and the others as subordinate minorities that enjoyed a lesser status and rights, similar to those accorded to the Chinese minorities elsewhere in the region. They had to educate them to view Singapore not as a Chinese city state, a Third China, but as a multi-racial polity that belonged equally to all its ethnic components.

In this regard, the PAP rulers considered the Barisan Sosialis, which then functioned as the chief patron and instigator of Chinese chauvinism and extremism, as the most formidable obstacle. They believed that so long as the Barisan Sosialis remained in existence and retained its ability to exploit the emotions of the Chinese on ethnic issues, they would find it extremely difficult to forge a national consensus — which included the Chinese majority — behind its founding principle of a multi-racial cultural democracy. They were also fearful that they themselves could get so bogged down with fighting battles against Barisan Sosialis, their chief political adversary, for the hearts and minds of the Singaporean Chinese that even their critically important objective of achieving rapid economic expansion and growth could be jeopardised. That would have inevitably made it much more difficult for them to manage Singapore's ethnic diversity successfully. It was essential for them to ensure that the Barisan Sosialis was only allowed a minimal role in the polity, if not being eliminated altogether.

The Barisan Sosialis was a powerful political organisation. When launched in July 1961 as a chauvinist-communist breakaway faction of the PAP, it had enjoyed "the support of an absolute majority of the Singapore electorate."[2] Based upon its noisy commitment to Chinese identity, language and education, heritage and culture, and its strong hold on the traditional voluntary associations of the Chinese, it clearly had the support of a significant majority within the Chinese community. The Chinese-educated had constituted its chief and powerful base.

The PAP rulers hastened the end of Barisan Sosialis by providing an effective administration that brought about rapid and impressive economic progress and by taking advantage of the laws introduced by the British that allowed it to impose curbs on the latter's ability to maintain its strong hold on the Chinese-educated masses. Already in the fateful election contest of September 1963, days before the new Federation of Malaysia had come into being, the PAP had defeated the Barisan Sosialis largely as a result of its impressive performance as the government during the preceding four years. The PAP, with a popular vote of 46.9 per cent, had secured 37 of the 51 seats in the legislature, while the Barisan Sosialis, having polled a third of the vote, had won only thirteen seats.

During the two years that Singapore had been a part of Malaysia, the Malay-controlled federal government had made it extremely difficult for the Barisan Sosialis to function effectively. At the time of separation in 1965, with many of its cadres and leaders in detention and with internal factionalism and in-fighting on the rise, it had already been fighting for its survival. As an organisation it was not in a state to compete effectively against the PAP and to continue to maintain its hold on the Chinese-educated masses. However, the PAP rulers had to continue to treat the threat from the Barisan Sosialis seriously. They believed that in an independent Singapore, they could find it politically more difficult than the Malaysian federal government — which, contrary to the PAP, did not have to rely on popular support in Singapore to stay in power — to control and curb the activities of the Barisan Sosialis.

The achievements of the PAP government in securing rapid economic expansion and progress had already begun to weaken the commitment of many Chinese to the Barisan Sosialis. In an expanding economy with increasing opportunities, not many Chinese were willing to be left out. Because of their traditional sense of pragmatism, an increasing number of the Chinese was beginning to feel reluctant to remain loyal to the Barisan Sosialis based only upon its strong defence and espousal of their Chineseness and of their language, education and culture. Furthermore, the Barisan Sosialis itself had begun to feel more dispirited following separation as it could no longer take advantage of the support and backing from the still powerful Socialist Front across the causeway in Malaysia; it was now virtually on its own in battling the PAP government.

Fortunately for the PAP, in December 1965 the organisation had taken the decision to boycott parliament. By late 1966, all Barisan Sosialis representatives had resigned from parliament and the party, totally ignoring the new objective Singapore reality and in a fit of foolishness, had chosen to follow the path of a mass struggle. Chan Heng Chee was to note later that by 1970

> . . . the Barisan Sosialis has been totally eclipsed. The major security actions against the party left the organisation without any effective leadership. Periodic arrests by the police of key men in the organisation, particularly those in charge of propaganda and cultural activities, have prevented the party from actual recovery.[3]

The Barisan Sosialis refused to participate in the 1968 general elections, thereby allowing the PAP to win all the 58 seats in parliament and establish itself virtually as the unchallenged national ruling party of Singapore. By 1970, it seemed that the party had chosen to wither away slowly without giving the PAP a real fight, thereby allowing the latter to pursue its agenda for the management of ethnicity without having to worry about a strong political opposition that drew considerable strength from Chinese chauvinism and extremism.

2. *Giving special recognition to the Malays*
The PAP rulers had to recognise the Malays, who constituted some fourteen per cent of the population, as the *bumiputra* and continue to accord them a special place and give them special treatment in a Singapore that had just been forced to establish itself as a sovereign independent republic. Following separation, there had been a great deal of anger, concern and fear among the Malays. A prominent Malay intellectual and activist told this writer recently:

> After the separation of Singapore from Malaysia, it was very difficult for the Malays psychologically to accept their reduced status of ethnic minority in a Singapore dominated by the Chinese majority. During the period of Malaysia, even though they were based in Singapore, they were an integral part of the indigenous ruling Malay majority. They were the kith and kin of the Malays across the causeway in Malaysia. The problem of their adjustment to an independent Singapore was accentuated by the fact that they were to be a minority in an island that was theirs and had remained *Tanah Melayu* to them even during the period of British rule, despite the fact that they themselves had wielded little power and influence at the time. Singapore was now to be ruled essentially by the Chinese whose powerful position in the island they had long resented. The disappointment and anger at their changed fortunes and the accompanying frustration continued into the 1970s.[4]

It was necessary for the PAP rulers to assure the Malays that Singapore's separation from Malaysia would make little real difference to their role and special position as the *bumiputra* and that they had nothing to fear as their special interests would remain protected as before.

The PAP rulers had little problem in continuing with formally according the Malays a special position. But they could not afford to introduce aspects of it that came into direct conflict with their founding principle of a multi-racial cultural democracy. As it was a founding principle, critically important for future ethnic harmony and Singapore's survival, they were keen to ensure that it remained sacrosanct, and was not compromised or undermined in any way. Therefore, to satisfy the indigenous Malays, they had to work out an arrangement that could be seen to accord them a special position but that, at the same time, did not compromise their own founding principle in any significant way. Article 152 (2) of the Constitution of Singapore stipulates:

> The Government shall exercise its functions in such manner as to recognise the special position of the Malays, who are the indigenous people of Singapore, and accordingly it shall be the responsibility of the Government to protect, safeguard, support, foster and promote their political, educational, religious, economic, social and cultural interests and the Malay language.

Article 153 further provides: "The Legislature shall by law make provision for regulating Muslim religious affairs and for constituting a Council to advise the President in matters relating to the Muslim religion."

These constitutional provisions could have been interpreted to allow the Malays such things as positive discrimination in their favour as to employment, business and industry, admission to educational institutions and promotion in public service. But in practice, during the following years, the PAP rulers did not offer the Malays, under the provisions, much more than the mere symbolic. Unlike the constitution of neighbouring Malaysia which spelled out the benefits and entitlements to be enjoyed by the Malays under its provisions relating to their special position, the Singapore Constitution had provided essentially a broad, vague commitment on the part of the government, to be interpreted and implemented by it as it wished. The Malays themselves could not claim any specific special privileges, treatment or entitlements based upon these constitutional provisions. As a part of the special position of the Malays, the PAP rulers accorded the Malay language the status of the sole national language. They based the symbols of the new state, the national anthem and the flag, on the Malays. They allowed free university education to Malay students.

The arrangement during the Malaysia period, on which this limited special position had been based, had been accepted by non-Malay Singaporeans largely because Singapore was then a part of Malaysia. The problem faced by the PAP rulers, therefore, was how to continue it in the new context of an independent Singapore without incurring the anger of the non-Malays, especially the Chinese, who now viewed themselves as full citizens of *their* independent Singapore. The unreasonable way Singapore had been treated while in Malaysia from 1963 to 1965, and the insulting manner in which it had been asked to separate, had generated considerable resentment and anger among most non-Malay Singaporeans. Therefore, they were not easily disposed to being generous to the Malays and continuing to accept their special position which in the new context of an independent Singapore seemed more special than during the period when Singapore was a part of Malaysia and when Singapore had little choice in the matter.

In real practical terms, from the beginning, the PAP rulers viewed the Malay special position only as a means of helping the community to develop capabilities, especially through education and training, that enabled its members to take as much advantage of available opportunities to earn a good living as their compatriots. Its symbolic aspects were of importance only during the first decade or so because then they gave the Malays the feeling that despite separation from Malaysia in 1965 they had remained formally recognised as the only *bumiputra*. In essence, the special position of the Malays in Singapore has remained limited to the domains of education and training. In 1964, when the Singaporean Malays, instigated largely by Malay leaders from across the causeway, had been noisily demanding a better deal from the PAP rulers, Prime Minister Lee Kuan Yew said that the Malays must be prepared to undergo training to become skilled technicians.[5] There were just not enough jobs for primary school leavers as messengers, peons and other similar unskilled work. He maintained: "Once the Malays are as well educated and qualified as the others, then their capacity to hold better jobs and have a better standard of living will automatically follow."[6] As we shall see later, this approach of the PAP rulers has been greatly successful in improving the position of the Malay community.

3. Adhering to the founding principle of a multi-racial cultural democracy

The PAP rulers had to adhere strictly to their founding principle of a multi-racial cultural democracy and allow the different ethnic components the fullest possible freedom in respect of their different cultures and ways of life, religions and values, and languages and educational institutions. In the past, following their assumption of power in 1959, they had shown themselves to be strong advocates of cultural integration. Anticipating the eventual merger of Singapore with Malaya, they had backed and promoted the idea of a national Malayan culture. They had even established a Ministry of Culture with the purpose to help shape a Malayan culture. The Minister of Culture and the leading ideologue in the PAP of the time, S Rajaratnam, had strongly argued the need for a Malayan culture in a series of articles that appeared in PAP's own official organ, *Petir*. He argued:

> For us the creation of a Malayan culture is a matter of practical politics. It is as essential for us to lay the foundations for a Malayan culture, as it is for us to build hospitals, schools and factories and provide jobs for our rapidly expanding population. Malayan culture is, for us, an essential part of nation-building.
>
> . . . In the Malayan context the cultural problem is but another aspect of our attempt to forge a nation out of a hotch-potch of racial and religious groups. We do not regard the creation of a Malayan culture simply as an academic problem because we are convinced that unless we weld the various races in Malaya into a national group, we make inevitable racial and religious conflicts . . .
>
> To ignore the ever-present danger of communal conflict is to live in a fool's paradise. We need only look at what has

happened in India, Ceylon, Indonesia, Thailand, Burma and what is happening in Africa and the Middle East to realise that racial conflicts are more widespread than we realise.[7]

However, after separation in 1965, the PAP rulers did not wish to stir up the hornet's nest unnecessarily by explicitly promoting cultural integration and bringing into existence a distinctive Singapore national culture. The heightened ethnic sensitivities and the more intensified concerns of the different ethnic segments with regard to their distinctive identities, languages and cultures had made it necessary for the PAP rulers to ensure that their own policies relating to management of ethnicity were seen to be geared to maintaining Singapore's cultural and linguistic diversity. Therefore, the integrative policies they considered necessary had either to be disguised or had to be designed in a way that they were not seen to be in conflict with their founding principle of a multi-racial cultural democracy.

Singapore with a population of only about 2.5 million came to have four official languages — Malay, Mandarin, English and Tamil. The government ensured that all official documents and notices were made available in the four languages. The parliament provided facilities for instantaneous translation to enable its members to debate in any of the four languages. Ethnic segments were allowed to produce and distribute newspapers and magazines in their own different languages freely. On the whole, unrestricted use of the different languages, for official as well as unofficial purposes, was permitted. The government-controlled television and radio services established special units to produce and transmit a variety of Chinese, Malay and Indian programmes in their own languages and reflecting their distinctive traditions, heritages, cultures and ways of life. The Mission Statement of the Television Corporation of Singapore commits itself to "reflect the diverse heritage of our society and help nurture the growing Singapore identity".

Even the four kinds of different schools, teaching through the media of Malay, Chinese, English and Tamil, were allowed to exist at first even though in the past they had only represented conflicting ethnic, social and political orientations and had tended to reinforce ethnic exclusivism. English- and most Chinese-medium schools were well-endowed and offered good education. But the Malay and Tamil schools, lacking the level of community support that the Chinese schools enjoyed, did not even provide acceptable education; they existed more to satisfy the emotional commitments of the two communities to their culture and language.

Many of these schools, especially the Chinese-medium schools, had functioned as strong centres of ethnic chauvinism and extremism. They had taught more about China and India than about Singapore. For example, most of the textbooks used in the Chinese schools, as well as many of the teachers, were imported from China. The PAP rulers were aware of the almost entirely China-based orientation of the products of the Chinese schools as these had formed a large part of the cadres as well as the mass backing of their party before these separated to form the Chinese chauvinist-communist Barisan Sosialis in 1961. But because of their founding principle of a multi-racial cultural democracy and practical political considerations, they could not just close down these institutions. The PAP rulers had to maintain their image as being committed to maintaining and sustaining Singapore's ethnic diversity and dispel any fears that the distinctive identities, languages and cultures of the different ethnic segments were being threatened in any way. At the same time, they had to try to get around the problem of these community-based schools. Thus they argued that the problems represented by these separate schools could be solved or ameliorated by improving their standards and facilities and changing the content and emphases of their education.

Furthermore, learning from the experience of other multi-racial societies in Asia, the PAP rulers placed special emphasis on ensuring that the various ethnic segments developed full confidence in the non-racialism and impartiality of the government, its agencies and personnel. From the beginning, the PAP government began to nurture and guard its ethnic image and credibility carefully and ensured that the PAP was recognised, in the words of its President Dr Toh Chin Chye, "not as a mere political party or as another political party, but (that we must be) recognised as a national political institution that draws support from all races and from different social sectors."[8] What was considered critical was that it was not viewed as an instrument of the dominant Chinese majority. Prime Minister Lee Kuan Yew and his colleagues in the government also sought to make sure that not only their policies were impartial and fair to all ethnic segments, but also that their administration by petty officials at the grassroots levels was free of any ethnic bias and discrimination. They tried to ensure that throughout, the integrity, incorruptibility and impartiality of the judiciary remained entirely beyond reproach.

The PAP rulers made sure that ethnic minorities secured fair representation at the highest levels of decision-making. Since independence, the composition of the cabinet, the ministry and the parliament has reflected the multi-ethnic character of Singapore. They have always had a reasonable number of Malays and Indians in highly visible positions as ministers. They have also shown willingness at times to compromise their strong commitment to the merit system to ensure some ethnic balance in public services personnel.

In all this, during this first phase of their management of ethnicity, the PAP rulers remained extremely concerned about the dangerous threat posed by ethnic extremism and chauvinism. They were also mindful of the fact that most Singaporeans belonged to immigrant families that had not lived in Singapore for long. There had been little in their treatment and role during the period of British rule that could have pursuaded them to develop a strong sense of attachment to Singapore. Isolation from one another and the different economic and other functions performed by them as communities had disabled them from developing a sense of a shared common history and destiny. They still looked, with a great deal of emotion, towards the lands of their forefathers — Malaya, China, Indonesia and India — as "home". It was, therefore, essential for the PAP rulers to ensure that their objective of a multi-racial cultural democracy was not turned into a strictly "separate but equal" approach that was "only capable of breeding not openness but chauvinism, and an affinity not to Singapore but a retrogressive identification with the lands and heritage of our respective forebears."[9]

It was thus essential for the first-generation PAP rulers to promote certain processes of ethnic integration. These had included both non-controversial elements, which did not detract from their founding principle of a multi-racial cultural democracy, and a more controversial programme that was aimed at turning the multi-lingual island into an essentially English-speaking Singapore.

Most of the non-controversial elements of the integrative programme of the PAP rulers had, in fact, been introduced earlier, soon after they had first assumed limited power in 1959.[10] Firstly, they had introduced a system of integrated schools which offered instruction through the medium of more than one language. The 1956 report of the All Party Committee on Chinese Education, which had first initiated the idea of integrated schools, said that "the greatest hope for multi-racial Singapore [is] to ensure that the younger generation grow up under the best conditions of intermingling. Everything should be done to break down mutual exclusiveness between the two streams of education — English and vernacular."[11] The integrated schools proved effective in bringing together pupils of different ethnic backgrounds within one school — studying and playing together and being able to develop mutual tolerance, understanding and respect. Before this, a vast majority of pupils, at all levels of schooling went to their own exclusive community schools, physically separated from schools of the other races. The integrated schools were the first to provide major institutionalised contact between the Malay, Chinese and Indian children.

Secondly, the new PAP government had set up a Ministry of Culture with the special purpose to promote "a national cultural pattern". They had created new state symbols, a new flag and anthem, in place of the British colonial ones. Each school day began with all students gathered together to sing the national anthem and to salute the flag. Later from 1966, they were further required daily to recite the following oath of loyalty to Singapore: "We the citizens of Singapore, pledge ourselves as one united people, regardless of race, language or religion, to build a democratic society based on justice and equality so as to achieve happiness, prosperity and progress for our nation." In 1970, the Ministry of Education introduced a set of history textbooks for primary schools in the four official languages that told "the story of the various immigrant races". The main characters in the books were the immigrants and the books extolled their values and their hard work and perseverance.[12]

Thirdly, in 1960, the government set up a Housing and Development Board (HDB) to deal with the acute problem of housing. In doing that, the HDB, from the beginning, chose to go beyond the mere purpose of providing good public housing at affordable (significantly below existing market value) prices. It created only integrated public housing estates that maintained a strict ethnic and social mix through its allocation policies. In 1989, in proposing legislation to enable the HDB to maintain a desired ethnic mix in its estates more effectively, S Dhanabalan, the minister in charge of public housing, described the problem in parliament as it had existed in 1960 when the board had been set up:

> [In] the late fifties and early sixties . . . various sections of our population at that time were gathered in different pockets distinguishable by their racial or dialect groups. The Malays, for example, were concentrated in Geylang Serai, Eunos and a few other areas. The Indians were gathered in the Serangoon Road and Naval Base areas. The Chinese were fragmented into dialect groups, each with its own enclave: the Cantonese in Kreta Ayer, the Hokkiens in Telok Ayer, the Teochews in the Upper Serangoon area and in Boat Quay, and the Hainanese in Beach Road/Middle Road.
>
> Each group was fiercely proud of its own identity and defended its narrow interests stoutly. Each clung to its own clan or dialect community for security. There was no social cohesion. We were a divided society.
>
> The massive public housing effort gave us the opportunity to mix the population. We made sure that every HDB new town and estate had a balanced mix of racial groups.[13]

The HDB has today grown into a gigantic organisation that provides integrated housing for some 86 per cent of Singapore's population and acts as a major instrument "in bringing all the races and social groups closer together, while allowing each group to practice its own beliefs and customs".[14] During the period from 1960 to 1980, a total of over 370,000 dwellings were constructed and made available by HDB.

Creating an English-Speaking Singapore

The more controversial objective of creating an essentially English-speaking Singapore had clearly constituted a central element of the integrative agenda of the PAP rulers. Their intent had seemed obvious then, but for practical political reasons it had not been spelled out explicitly. The objective may have seemed to reflect the natural preference of Prime Minister Lee Kuan Yew and his close associates because all of them were English-educated and highly westernised. They spoke their own community languages with little fluency and they did not have much close contact with the grassroots of their own communities. They essentially had worked and lived in the world of the highly westernised, English-educated colonial Singapore. The PAP rulers had, however, more compelling reasons to pursue the objective.

Firstly, having committed themselves to a multi-racial Singapore that allowed its diverse ethnic segments the freedom to retain their distinctiveness, and in consequence their separateness, they considered their desire to create an essentially English-speaking Singapore as vitally necessary to facilitate communication and intermingling among the different peoples and to enable them all "to fuse some of their elements into a national cultural pattern".

Secondly, they strongly believed that a transfer of leadership and power through normal democratic processes into the hands of the "backward-looking and non-modernising" non-English-educated, especially the Chinese-educated, was extremely damaging to Singapore's ethnic, economic, political and international interests. Thus they considered it as their special obligation to their new nation to ensure that power remained vested in the hands of the modernising English-educated leadership. The creation of an essentially English-speaking

Singapore was seen as the single most effective way of denying the leadership role and power to the Chinese-educated.

Thirdly, they believed that an essentially English-speaking Singapore would give it the image of a cosmopolitan international city and help disguise that much more its distinctive Chineseness, thereby making it less unacceptable to its powerful Malay neighbours.

Fourthly, they were confident that an essentially English-speaking Singapore would inevitably offer a much less fertile ground for the growth of Chinese chauvinism, which they considered to constitute one of the most dangerous threats to the future of their new nation.

Finally, they were certain that it would give Singapore a level of access to modern knowledge, science and technology necessary for it to achieve continuing economic growth and prosperity.

It is important to recognise here that even though at first Prime Minister Lee Kuan Yew and his close associates sought to create an essentially English-speaking Singapore, based upon the existing ethnic and regional geo-political realities, they were obviously not unmindful of its negative, deculturising influence on their peoples. The PAP rulers were all highly educated, well-read and sophisticated intellectuals. They could not easily be accused of a crudity like attempting to turn Singaporeans into yellow and brown sahibs, shorn of their identity and enervated through the loss of their cultural moorings, heritage and values. Prime Minister Lee Kuan Yew himself at the time had sent his own children first to Chinese-medium schools. The desire of the PAP rulers to create an essentially English-speaking Singapore thus has to be viewed in relation to their founding principle of a multi-racial cultural democracy in which all the different ethnic segments were guaranteed the right to be able to maintain and enhance their distinctive identities, cultures, languages and traditional values. Prime Minister Lee Kuan Yew told this writer in February 1969:

> ... I do not want an only English-educated community. It is not only language. With the language goes the literature, proverbs, folklore, beliefs, value patterns. It is useful for

> Singapore to use and continue using the English language because it provides continuity in the records, administration, law and the medium in which all the various racial groups compete at par with each other . . .
>
> But apart from that, . . . there is the spiritual and cultural side of life. The Singaporean, whether he is of ethnic Chinese, Indian or Malay descent, has his own culture. Over the centuries something distinctive may emerge, something separate from China, India, or Indonesia, or Britain. However, if in the interim you deculturise a person, erase his own culture when you have not got something as relevant to put in its place, then you have enervated him. The importance therefore of this lifeline with the past.[15]

Referring to experiences in his own family, he had elaborated:

> I find it interesting watching my nephews and nieces and my own children — the difference between those who are effectively bilingual and those who are not. Some of them, like my own children, are in Chinese-language schools where English is the second language. My wife and I were confident they would master English. The difference between their cousins and them who are in Chinese language schools and those of their cousins in English language schools where Chinese is the second language is very marked. That those in Chinese language schools have tremendous self-confidence, may be completely unfounded. But they are conscious that their cultural heritage goes back 4,000 years, that a "Lee" (Lee Yen) was the first emperor of the glorious Tang dynasty from the seventh to the tenth century B.C.
>
> It's much like what my Indian colleague told me — that his own children tutored in English and at the same time in the South Indian language, culture and history, know that their ancestors, the "Nairs", were great warriors. This gives them a great aplomb, confidence and cultural ballast . . .
>
> If we are going to make our own distinctive contribution to civilised and cultivated living in Southeast Asia, then we must have this cultural ballast.[16]

At least, Prime Minister Lee Kuan Yew had obviously believed that in order to be good citizens, Singaporeans needed to retain their distinctive identities and cultural moorings to a great extent. It was also thought that most Singaporeans in the past had shown such deep commitment to their traditional cultures and heritages that it was not very likely that many of their children would become excessively deculturised through western influences.

In pursuing the unspoken objective of creating an English-speaking Singapore, the PAP rulers had to be extremely careful that it was not seen as moving the country in a direction different from that clearly implied by their founding principle of a multi-racial cultural democracy. They had to ensure that it did not in any way damage or erode the ability of the various ethnic segments to maintain and sustain their distinctive identities, languages and cultures, for that would inevitably attract a strong reaction from them and create an ethnic controversy damaging to the PAP rulers' integrative agenda. They knew that there was considerable concern among the Chinese, especially the Chinese-educated, about the unspoken agenda as the latter were certain that its effect was to be felt largely by members of their community, whose distinctive Chinese linguistic and cultural identity would inevitably become markedly diluted, if not lost altogether.

The wish to create an essentially English-speaking Singapore was pursued chiefly through the PAP government's education and language policies. Even though Chinese, Malay, English and Tamil all enjoyed the status of official languages, English became the first official language from the beginning, with the other languages enjoying only a symbolic status. English remained the language of the administration and the courts. As the economy began to be internationalised, its use in trade and industry increased correspondingly. It also remained the chief language of instruction, in schools as well as tertiary institutions. It was clearly expected by Prime Minister Lee Kuan Yew and his colleagues that in the long run English would become the chief language of most Singaporeans.

To make English more easily acceptable as the chief language and to enable Singaporeans to retain their distinctive languages and cultures, the PAP rulers soon introduced a significantly modified concept of bilingualism as a cornerstone of their education policy. Originally, bilingualism introduced by them in 1959 had meant that every pupil learnt the national language, Malay, and either English, Mandarin or Tamil depending on the language stream of the school. The modified system as introduced in 1966 substituted the national language, Malay, with English and made study of either Malay, Mandarin or Tamil compulsory depending in almost all cases on which represented the mother tongue of the pupil.

This was also expected to bring about, over the years, the replacement by bilingual schools of Chinese, Malay and Tamil schools, which were then viewed as sources of ethnic chauvinism and as a serious obstacle in the way of PAP's integrative agenda. Under the bilingual scheme introduced in 1966, all school pupils had to learn one of the other official languages, in addition to English, as a part of the official curriculum. It was ensured that the second language that was learnt by almost all Chinese and Malay pupils was their mother tongue.

The traditional English-medium schools were redesignated as English-stream schools that taught Mandarin, Malay or Tamil as a compulsory second language. Similarly, the schools of the Chinese, Malay and Indian communities, which used their own community languages as the media of instruction, were turned respectively into Chinese-stream, Malay-stream and Tamil-stream schools providing compulsory instruction in English as a second language.

Talking about bilingualism, Prime Minister Lee Kuan Yew proudly told this writer in February 1969:

> There is no boy or girl in a Singapore school today who is monolingual or taught to be monolingual. Whether they are effectively bilingual or trilingual depends upon their innate ability, their application and the quality of the teaching. Our policy is designed to make it impossible for anybody to get through the compulsory eight years of education without at least exposure to a second language, literature and culture. So nobody can believe that his own language and culture is the beginning and the end of the world. The

parents decide whether they send their children to an English-language school in which they will also learn their own mother tongue, be it Chinese, Tamil or Malay, or they send their children to a Chinese or Tamil or Malay language school, where the second language taught will be English.[17]

Prime Minister Lee Kuan Yew and his colleagues had also expected that their policy of bilingualism would enable the different peoples to understand each other and develop respect for their distinctive cultures and heritages. Prime Minister Lee Kuan Yew underlined its importance to this writer in February 1969:

> There must also be the acknowledgement that no single ethnic group has a monopoly of wisdom and genius. And it is salutary thought for our children to know that their friends, be they Chinese, Indians, Malays or Eurasians that there are other languages and literatures, other civilisations as great if not greater than that of their ancestors. For example, when a Chinese boy learns that his Tamil schoolmate has a language and literature which goes back beyond 3,000 years, he stops to think that Chinese history and civilisation are not the beginning and end of human history and civilisation. He is then aware that his is only one of several great civilisations in the world. I think this breeds an atmosphere of humility and tolerance, without at the same time being apologetic over one's own background. They know that they are not inadequate, that when the Europeans were still in hunting communities in the forests of Western Europe, living in caves, there were well cultivated settlements along the Yellow and Indus rivers. But introvert smugness, and a few centuries of industrial and technological discovery and progress, have put the Europeans and Americans well ahead of them.[18]

The bilingual education policy was more firmly established in 1969 when the second language began to be included as an examination subject for the School Certificate Examinations.

The primacy of English and the turning of Singapore into an

essentially English-speaking entity was achieved more easily and quickly than expected. It had been considerably facilitated by the natural inclination of parents, representing all the different ethnic segments, to take the pragmatic decision of sending their children to English-medium schools in preference to the community-based schools that used Chinese, Malay or Tamil as the medium of instruction. In this, a significant contribution had also been made by the government's own economic policies that were geared to creating a modern industrial and scientific community in Singapore. Many in Singapore had then been surprised by the ease with which increasing numbers of parents, especially Chinese, had begun readily, and willingly, to subordinate their deep emotional attachment to their community-based educational institutions (which in the past had been one of the most important promoters of their different languages and cultures) to the practical need to secure for their children the education and training which was the best and which prepared them most effectively for higher education or the job market. As can seen in Tables 5 and 6, the change was extremely dramatic.

Even though this remarkable change in parental preference was noticed by the PAP rulers, they did not choose to take any remedial action beyond their existing policy of bilingualism to deal with the lessened ability of pupils of different ethnic backgrounds to retain their traditional values and cultural moorings; to them then it possibly was a welcome change. Prime Minister Lee Kuan Yew told this writer in February 1969:

> ... the statistics over the last decade indicate a trend for the parents to choose the English-language schools where opportunities for higher education, particularly at university level, in Singapore and abroad, are highest. So they get the best of both worlds — emotional satisfaction at continuity of culture and tradition, the ability to read their ancestral tablets and, equally if not more important, the ability to get on with the business of earning a living in Singapore.[19]

Table 5: *School Enrolments, 1959, 1972 and 1985*

(in per cent)

Medium of Instruction	1959	1972	1985
English	50.9	64.8	97.0
Chinese	43.6	30.9	3.0
Malay	5.0	4.0	–
Tamil	0.5	0.3	–

Source: Department of Statistics

Table 6: *Primary School Enrolments, 1972 and 1982*

(in per cent)

Medium of Instruction	1972	1982
English	64.66	88.52
Chinese	31.71	11.36
Malay	3.35	0.10
Tamil	0.27	–

Source: Department of Statistics

To start with, to the PAP rulers the bilingual programme, in line with their objective of turning Singapore into an essentially English-speaking entity, must have seemed to have achieved exceptional success. In any case, they had been certain that even in the case of the large number of pupils who had switched to English-medium schools, the bilingual education policy would serve them well in retaining their cultural moorings through the compulsory teaching of their mother tongue. Later, however, experience proved that the compulsory teaching of mother tongue as a second language (including making it an examination subject) was not adequate to ensure that these students were able to retain their cultural moorings and traditional values in a substantial way.

The PAP rulers obviously had made a miscalculation in placing their reliance almost entirely on the capacity of bilingual education to enable pupils of all races to maintain their own distinctive cultural moorings and to produce intermingling and understanding of each other. As we noted earlier, the policy had resulted in the continuing decline of the Chinese-medium, Malay-medium and Tamil-medium schools, their place being taken by the English-stream schools. More and more students were being educated through the medium of English. On the whole, the policy had resulted chiefly in establishing an almost total supremacy of English. The PAP government itself had not taken long to give recognition to the *fait accompli*: in 1983, it announced that by 1987 all schools would have to switch to English as the first language, thus in effect making it the sole medium of instruction at all levels. It maintained that it had just found out that less than one per cent of those eligible for starting schooling had enrolled in Chinese-medium primary schools, and none in Malay-medium and Tamil-medium primary schools.

The supremacy of English and English-stream schools had begun to widen the spread of western values, way of life and attitudes rapidly among young Singaporeans and caused considerable erosion in their commitment to their different languages, cultures and heritages. They were increasingly being influenced by the rapidly westernising environment of Singapore which had a serious negative side to it. A large new class of "the ugly Singaporean" had emerged that showed little regard for Asian values. Ho Wing Meng, a Singapore teacher of philosophy, lamented about the change recently:

> Increasingly, acquisitiveness has become the very soul of society, penetrating almost every aspect of social life and thought. Everything has a price attached to it, so much so that Singaporeans, especially during the 1970s when the economy grew by leaps and bounds, appeared to be fast developing a system of values according to which the worth or significance of any person, object or activity was calculated exclusively in terms of his or its potential or actual pecuniary value. It was the market value (an expression which was used with increasing frequency) of any person, his services or his goods in terms of dollars and cents which mattered most; and anything which was not reducible to such quantitative terms (for example love, courage, honour, sacrifice, integrity, selflessness, each with

its irreducible qualitative wholeness) was largely ignored or at best regarded with mild contempt . . .

Once the rich had set the trend in conspicuous consumption and competitive methods of enhancing their prestige, it was only a matter of time before the middle-income group began to emulate their lifestyles.[20]

The government believed that the greatest impact of westernisation was felt within the Chinese community. Its impact on the Indians was seen as being extremely limited. As for the Malays, the government did not believe any special problem had been created. The issue had generated little concern and controversy within the community itself as most of its members clearly seemed to continue to retain their traditional commitment to their Malayness and their language, culture and religion.

Naturally, strong voices of concern emerged first within the Chinese community, especially among the Chinese-speaking. They had begun to fear that the increasing dominance of the English language and the fast-growing influence of westernisation would inevitably lead to the enervation of the Chinese community through their deculturisation. Starting from the mid-1970s, there was widespread public discussion and debate in Singapore, all lamenting at the erosion of traditional Asian values and the spread of western materialism and individualism. Prime Minister Lee Kuan Yew himself became so concerned about the consequences of the trend that in 1978 he chose to make a personal appeal to parents asking them not to abandon the Chinese-stream, Malay-stream and Tamil-stream schools in favour of the English-stream schools. He feared that, if unchecked, the trend was inevitably to threaten the survival of Singapore's Asian languages, cultures and values. A Singaporean academic has written that:

> . . . the government began to be concerned with the adverse effects of heightened individualism, leading — as it believed — to the erosion of moral and ethical values on the one hand and on the other to the loss of cultural identity . . . rampant individualism was seen as a threat to the family, in particular to the value of filial piety. With the spread of

English-medium education, there was the fear that young Singaporeans might lose their cultural moorings or, worse still, fall victim to certain deleterious influences emanating from the West. Implicitly, the preference was for the strengthening of group values as a basis for the attainment of social and economic well-being and the downgrading of self-centredness.[21]

There was thus, during the late 1970s, clear recognition both among the first-generation leaders of the PAP and the Chinese-speaking that the policies geared to creating an essentially English-speaking Singapore had been very successful, but were not necessarily for the good of Singapore. They had at least been detrimental to the interests of the Chinese community. The PAP leaders also realised that the policy of bilingual education had proved ineffective in limiting the impact of English-medium education on young Singaporeans and in assisting them, through the compulsory teaching of the mother tongue as a second language, to maintain a balance between the inevitable tide of westernisation and their own distinctive Asian cultures and values. The increasing pace and extent of westernisation had begun to pose a serious threat not only to the languages and cultures of the different ethnic segments, especially the Chinese, but also to the ability of Singaporeans to continue to achieve substantial economic expansion and progress in the future.

The result was that, during the late 1970s, Prime Minister Lee Kuan Yew and his first-generation colleagues began a dramatic shift in the application of their broad-based founding principle of a multi-racial cultural democracy. It represented an attempt once again to relate the founding principle of cultural democracy to the new realities of the Singapore of the late 1970s, resulting from a decade of spectacular economic progress and prosperity and the government's success in creating an English-speaking Singapore.

Notes

1. In 1948, the Indians, representing some seven per cent of the population, comprised so much as 45.3 per cent of the registered electorate, while the Chinese, accounting for over 75 per cent of the population, accounted for only 25.1 per cent of the electorate. Thomas J Bellows, *The People's Action Party of Singapore: Emergence of a Dominant Party System*, Yale University Southeast Asia Series, Monograph Series No. 14, 1970, p. 68.
2. *Ibid.*, pp. 75–6.
3. Chan Heng Chee, *The Dynamics of One Party Dominance*, Singapore 1978, p. 198.
4. Interview with a prominent Malay intellectual and activist, Singapore, September 1993.
5. Quoted in Alex Josey, *Lee Kuan Yew*, Singapore 1968, p. 92.
6. *Ibid.*, p. 92.
7. "Malayan Culture in the Making", *Petir*, Vol. III, No. 15, 7 September 1960, reproduced in Chan Heng Chee and Obaid ul Haq (editors), *S Rajaratnam: The Prophetic and the Political*, Singapore 1987, pp. 119–20. It may be useful to note that despite a dramatic change in the PAP's attitude during the past two decades, Rajaratnam has remained firmly wedded to the notion of a national culture.
8. Quoted in Chan Heng Chee, *The Dynamics of One Party Dominance*, Singapore 1978, p. 223.
9. K R Ramakrishna, "Singapore United", *The Straits Times*, Weekly Overseas Edition, 14 July 1990.
10. These had largely been based upon the 1956 report of the All Party Committee on Chinese Education appointed by the Singapore Legislative Assembly.
11. Quoted in Tham Seong Chee, "The Perception and Practice of Education", K S Sandhu and Paul Wheatley (editors), *Management of Success: The Moulding of Modern Singapore*, Singapore 1989, p. 495.
12. S Gopinathan, "Towards a National Educational System", in Riaz Hassan (editor), *Singapore: Society in Transition*, Oxford 1976, p. 74.
13. Quoted in Ooi Giok Ling, Sharon Siddique and Soh Kay Cheng, *The Management of Ethnic Relations in Public Housing Estates*, The Institute of Policy Studies, Singapore 1993, p. 10.
14. *Ibid.*, p. 11.
15. Interview with Lee Kuan Yew, Singapore, February 1969.
16. *Ibid.*
17. *Ibid.*
18. *Ibid.*
19. *Ibid.*
20. Ho Wing Meng, "Value Premises Underlying the Transformation of Singapore", in K S Sandhu and Paul Wheatley (editors), *Management of Success: The Moulding of Modern Singapore*, Singapore 1989, p. 678.
21. Tham Seong Chee, "The Perception and Practice of Education", in K S Sandhu and Paul Wheatley (editors), *ibid.*, p. 482.

CHAPTER 5

Asianising Singapore:
The Second Phase, 1979–90

A dramatic shift in the application of their founding principle of cultural democracy was signalled by the PAP rulers in 1979 when they inaugurated the "Speak Mandarin Campaign". The campaign, by itself, did not signify a dramatic change. Its importance lay in the fact that it represented the beginning of a new, second phase in the PAP government's management of ethnicity geared chiefly to, what in its totality meant, Asianising Singapore, including restoring the Chineseness of the Chinese. It did not mean turning the clock back and undoing entirely the making of an essentially English-speaking Singapore that had represented the main thrust of their strategy during the first phase. English was so well established, and acceptable to an increasing majority of its population, as the first language of administration, education and much of business, banking and industry, that there was little chance of its importance and usage being radically reduced. In 1984, the government officially designated English as the sole medium of education at all levels.

The second phase represented an attempt by the PAP rulers to restore and strengthen the moorings of the different peoples of Singapore in their different cultures and heritages so that they would be able to function with equal confidence in both the traditional worlds of their own respective communities as well as the western world of science and technology and international trade. The idea was to get Singaporeans to acquire and take advantage of the best of the two worlds.

Ironically the push for this significant change in direction had come from Prime Minister Lee Kuan Yew, who possibly was the most westernised of the first-generation leaders of the PAP. According to a Chinese-educated PAP leader, during the 1970s Prime Minister Lee Kuan Yew had come to develop extreme fears of Singaporeans, especially the Chinese, losing their distinctive Asian values, cultures and heritages:

> Senior Minister Lee had gone to one of the Commonwealth Prime Ministers' Conferences in the Bahamas during the seventies. There he was deeply influenced by the position of the blacks he saw. They spoke only English, even though in their own distinctive way. They did not know who they were. They had no language of their own and they had little left of their own culture, heritage and values. Upon his return, Prime Minister Lee was determined not to have that happen in Singapore. That is how he had come to initiate the Speak Mandarin Campaign. Later was to come the push for Confucianism. It was all geared to especially maintaining the culture, heritage and values of the Chinese.[1]

The Speak Mandarin Campaign could possibly have passed for an initiative of the PAP government of interest only to the Chinese community and not affecting the role and status of the Malays and the Indians. During the following years, however, it was followed by a number of other initiatives which cumulatively constituted the government's agenda for Asianising Singapore and which created considerable suspicion and concern among the non-Chinese minorities. These included: the introduction of the Religious Knowledge curriculum, the Special Assistance Plan (SAP) schools project, and the search for a national ideology and core values.

Furthermore, the fact that these initiatives coincided with the increasing assertiveness of the Chinese and the change in their attitudes with regard to the role and status of their community in Singapore ensured that these initiatives came to be seen, at least by the non-Malays and many English-educated Chinese, as measures seeking to appease the Chinese-speaking. Many non-Chinese even began to fear that these could eventually lead to an erosion of the equality of status accorded to the different racial groups under the founding principle of a multi-racial cultural democracy and allow the Chinese to establish their community as being more equal than others.

Some fifteen years had elapsed since the traumatic and threatening events of the forced separation of Singapore from Malaysia. Since independence, there had been no manifestations of any serious disharmony and conflict between the Chinese, the dominant majority, and the indigenous Malays and the Indians. President Sukarno had passed away and, by the late 1970s, Indonesia was firmly ruled by General Suharto, who had built up a strongly pragmatic regime that had preoccupied itself with the mammoth task of reconstructing the country's economy that had been savagely damaged through the excesses and total mismanagement of the era of Guided Democracy. Similarly, in Malaysia, during the 1970s, following the May 1969 general elections and the communal explosion, power had come to be wielded by Malay leaders, who notwithstanding their noisy pro-Malay rhetoric were disposed to placing the achievement of national economic growth and prosperity above everything else. At the beginning of the decade, in 1971, the Malay leaders had launched a New Economic Policy with the objective to give the indigenous Malays their fair share of economic power and wealth. They were aware that the only politically feasible way this radical redistribution of wealth and economic power could be achieved was by ensuring that there was continuing economic expansion and growth.

The geopolitical environment in the region had clearly changed dramatically. The regional organisation, Association of Southeast Asian Nations (ASEAN), had been built up on the basis of "partnership in progress and prosperity". Singapore had developed good relations with its large neighbours and partners in ASEAN, Indonesia and Malaysia. Its existence as a separate, sovereign entity was fully recognised and accepted by its neighbours. Singapore did not feel threatened. In view of these changes, it did not seem necessary for Singapore any more to continue to de-emphasise and disguise its Chineseness to the extent that it had been compelled to since 1965, following separation from Malaysia.

Furthermore, the spectacular economic progress and prosperity of the past fifteen years had given its chief architects, the Singaporean Chinese, a new sense of confidence. They saw no reason any more to continue to be overly cautious and prudent and not seek to openly assert themselves as a community, as the dominant majority. Following Singapore's separation, they had shown all the necessary consideration and sensitivity to the minorities, the indigenous Malays and the Indians, and had readily agreed to accord them an equal status and allowed them to maintain their languages, cultures and religions. Many amongst them had come to feel that it was time for the minorities to show understanding and recognise the special position of the Chinese as the dominant majority and the chief creators of a prosperous, modern Singapore.

Even the electoral equation for the PAP rulers had changed dramatically. During the early 1960s, Prime Minister Lee Kuan Yew and his first-generation colleagues had to depend substantially on the votes of ethnic minorities and the English-educated Chinese to maintain their hold on power. Many of the Chinese-speaking, who represented a significantly large part of the Chinese community, had remained loyal to the Chinese chauvinist Barisan Sosialis. At the time of separation in 1965, impressed by the zeal and commitment with which Singapore had been ruled by the PAP and the successes it had achieved in modernising and expanding its economy, the Chinese-educated had only just begun to shed their natural lack of affinity with its English-educated and highly westernised leadership. Thus, the support of the minorities and the English-educated Chinese had continued to remain critically important to the PAP rulers. They could not afford to alienate the indigenous Malays nor the Indians.

But by the late 1970s, the spectacular economic growth and prosperity achieved during the preceding fifteen years or so had dramatically changed the political equation for the PAP. The Barisan Sosialis had disappeared from the political scene and its place had not been taken by another credible opposition organisation. Since the 1968 general elections, the PAP had enjoyed a virtual monopoly of political power by continuing to win all seats in parliament. In view of the inability of any opposition representatives to secure election to parliament, the PAP had even chosen to create an opposition of its own in parliament by asking its back-bench members to perform the functions of an opposition. The PAP had clearly established itself as the unchallenged national party of Singapore, its natural ruler. During the 1970s, it had achieved considerable success in wooing the Chinese-educated and building a large, solid base of support within the Chinese community. This had naturally reduced the previously critical importance of the minorities' vote to the PAP. It had now begun to be far more crucial for the PAP to maintain its large electoral base within the Chinese community than to worry continually about ensuring that the Malay and Indian minorities remained satisfied with PAP rule and that their support remained substantially undiminished.

Thus, it was now imperative for the PAP rulers to start giving special attention to the concerns of the Chinese community. Already serious expressions of dissatisfaction within the Chinese community had begun to emerge. Firstly, there was growing concern being expressed with regard to the damaging effect of the PAP government's agenda of creating an essentially English-speaking Singapore. It was being viewed as the chief cause of the erosion in the commitment of increasing numbers of Chinese to their distinctive identity, language, culture, heritage and values.

Secondly, there was increasing dissatisfaction with the fact that since independence in 1965, little special recognition had been accorded to the Chinese as the dominant majority and as the chief creators of Singapore's rapidly increasing wealth and prosperity. On the other hand, Nanyang University, the powerful symbol of Chinese education, culture and heritage in Singapore, was faced with the prospect of closure at the hands of the PAP government during this time. A Singaporean educationist recently commented that the Speak Mandarin Campaign was "a balancing move to reassure the Chinese community that their cohesiveness, cultural identity, and language claims still remained a primary concern of the government."[2]

The PAP rulers knew that their entirely unchallenged

monopoly of political power could not last for ever. Vastly improved standards of living and access to mass media had begun to raise the political consciousness of Singaporeans and give them a greater understanding of the wider world and a new perspective on their own society and its polity. They were increasingly becoming a part of the modern world. There was a much greater awareness among them of being citizens of a modern, affluent democracy. Many among them had begun to raise questions about the dangers of a single political party enjoying a virtual monopoly of political power and being able to take for granted the electoral backing of Singaporeans. Some had even openly expressed resentment against what they saw as the increasing arrogance and cockiness of the government and its bureaucracy. Others had talked of the necessity to have some opposition representation, even if minimal, in parliament to act as a check on the PAP government. Taking advantage of these concerns, a more popularly-based opposition party, the Workers' Party, had begun to emerge under the leadership of J B Jeyaretnam; in 1981, Jeyaretnam was elected to parliament as the first opposition member in thirteen years when he defeated the PAP candidate in the Anson by-election.

This was the setting for the inauguration of the Speak Mandarin Campaign, a measure that heralded the beginning of the attempt by the PAP rulers to Asianise Singapore. Interestingly, the overall objective of Asianising Singapore was mostly carried out by the highly westernised second-generation leaders of the PAP who had grown up during the first phase of the PAP government's management of ethnicity when it was especially committed to creating an essentially English-speaking Singapore. In 1978, the prestigious *Report on the Ministry of Education*, produced by the influential Deputy Prime Minister, Dr Goh Keng Swee, had acknowledged: "With the large-scale movement to education in English, the risk of deculturisation cannot be ignored."[3]

Launching the Speak Mandarin Campaign on 7 September 1979, Prime Minister Lee Kuan Yew argued that if the Chinese continued to use their dialects, English would become the common language between the Chinese representing different dialect groups. He said:

> Chinese Singaporeans face a dilemma. The Chinese we speak is divided among more than twelve dialects. Children at home speak dialect; in school they learn English and Mandarin. After 20 years of bilingual schooling, we know that very few children can cope with two languages plus one dialect, certainly not much more than the twelve per cent that make it to junior colleges. The majority have ended up speaking English and dialect.[4]

Five years later, again launching the year's Speak Mandarin Campaign on 21 September 1984, Prime Minister Lee Kuan Yew said that the government did not necessarily have to launch the campaign. It could have allowed the language habits of Singaporeans to evolve freely. "Then I fear the use of dialects will persist with not Amoy but pidgin Hokkien becoming most common, and Mandarin restricted to the classrooms. That is totally unacceptable."[5]

To start with, the chief purpose of the Speak Mandarin Campaign was to promote the use of Mandarin by the Chinese in place of their many different dialects. The government had collected a great deal of data in early 1979 relating to languages and dialects used by Singaporeans in dealing with bus drivers and conductors and at food stalls in hawker centres. The government wished to discourage the use of Chinese dialects strongly and promote Mandarin as the common language of all the Chinese. The Prime Minister had projected that once it was clear to the government that Chinese parents wanted their children to learn and use Mandarin, not dialects, the government would take administrative action to ensure that their desire was fulfilled.

> All government officers, including those in hospitals and clinics, and especially those in manning counters, will be instructed to speak Mandarin except to the elderly, those over 60. All Chinese taxi-drivers, bus conductors and hawkers will be required to pass an oral Mandarin test, or to attend Mandarin classes to make them adequate and competent to understand and speak Mandarin to their customers.[6]

Unfortunately, in all this, the government did not show much special concern that the Speak Mandarin Campaign could easily be misinterpreted or misunderstood by the Malays and the Indians as de-emphasising the importance of the distinctive languages and cultures of the minorities.

Soon it became clear that the purposes behind the Speak Mandarin Campaign were far more important and far-reaching. The PAP rulers began to present English and Mandarin as being equally important: the importance of English lay in giving Singaporeans access to modern science and technology, and of Mandarin in providing the Chinese the crucial key to their culture, heritage and values. In 1984, Prime Minister Lee Kuan Yew, while launching that year's Speak Mandarin Campaign, said that English could not be emotionally acceptable to the Chinese as their mother tongue. He argued:

> To have no emotionally acceptable language as our mother tongue is to be emotionally crippled. We shall doubt ourselves. We shall be less self-confident. Mandarin is emotionally acceptable as our mother tongue. It also unites the different dialect groups. It reminds us that we are part of an ancient civilisation with an unbroken history of over 5,000 years. This is a deep and strong psychic force, one that gives confidence to a people to face up to and overcome great changes and challenges . . .
>
> . . . Therefore, I can state that its psychological value cannot be over-emphasised. Parents want their children to be successful. They also want their children to retain traditional Chinese values in filial piety, loyalty, benevolence and love. Through Mandarin their children can emotionally identify themselves as part of an ancient civilisation whose continuity was because it was founded on a tried and tested value system.[7]

Clearly, the chief objective of the Speak Mandarin Campaign was to promote Mandarin as a common language among the Chinese so that they were able to have renewed and fuller access to their culture, heritage and values and that, as a result, they were able to retain and enhance their Chineseness.

The campaign had been organised by the PAP government especially for the Chinese community as the various unwholesome aspects of westernisation had been felt the most among the Chinese. Much greater deculturisation had been occurring among the English-educated Chinese than among any of the other peoples, the Malays and the Indians. In the case of the Malays and the Indians, their culture, heritage and values had not come under any similar threat and therefore the government did not feel that they required any remedial action initiated by the government such as a Speak Malay Campaign or a Speak Tamil Campaign. However, many among the Malays and the Indians, representing small and essentially powerless minorities facing a large and dominant Chinese majority, were strongly sensitive to and fearful of anything special being done for the Chinese by the government. Some of them had come to have an entirely irrational fear that it was a part of a larger, hidden agenda to create a Chinese Singapore. A Singapore academic, close to the government, reported soon afterwards that the Malays, Indians and Eurasians "feel threatened and perhaps even alienated by the repeated exhortation to speak Mandarin, and they also become more aware of their minority status as a result".[8] Brigadier-General Lee Hsien Loong, a senior minister in the government, acknowledged these fears later while speaking at the Speak Mandarin Campaign Launching Ceremony in October 1988 and sought to reassure the minorities that they had nothing to fear:

> The Speak Mandarin Campaign is not meant to make Singapore a more Chinese society, at the expense of the Malays and Indians. It is meant to make dialect-speaking Chinese replace dialect with Mandarin. Malay and Indian Singaporeans are fortunate that they do not face a problem of dialects as Chinese Singaporeans do. But the mother tongue and traditional values are as important to them as Mandarin is to the Chinese.
> . . . Our desire to preserve traditional values is not confined to the Chinese community alone. It is good for the nation that Singaporeans of all races have a clear sense of

where they have come from, and why they are here. Each community should take pride in its heritage, retain it and develop upon it.[9]

Soon after launching the Speak Mandarin Campaign, the PAP government sought to widen and strengthen religious education in schools. The *Report on Moral Education, 1979* had already acknowledged the important role that religious studies played in promoting moral values among Singaporeans. For some time, the government accepted Bible Knowledge and Islamic Religious Knowledge as examination subjects. In 1982, it extended the Religious Knowledge curriculum for upper secondary level students. Dr Goh Keng Swee, First Deputy Prime Minister and Minister of Education, announced that Confucian Ethics would be made available as one of the options.

A group of Confucian scholars from the United States and Taiwan were invited to Singapore by the government in August 1982 for three weeks of discussions, lectures and consultations. During the visit of these scholars, the Singaporean mass media, as if on cue, were full of Confucianism. Wherever Singaporeans, including the non-Chinese, gathered, they talked of Confucianism. The eminent overseas scholars agreed with the government's view that the preponderance of the Chinese in Singapore's population made it justifiable to introduce the teachings of Confucianism as one of the options in the Religious Knowledge curriculum. One of the visiting scholars, Professor Hsu Cho Yun, argued that it was important to distinguish Confucianism from Chineseness as it had "already crossed national borders and gone over the boundaries of ethnic identity".[10] Interestingly, having watched the excessive preoccupation of the Singapore mass media with Confucianism, even he acknowledged that the non-Chinese in Singapore "worry that Confucianism may be used by the government to displace other religions. They are also concerned that Chinese chauvinism may eventually dominate other groups."[11] Hsu sought to assure them that Confucianism was "a universal system of ethics and a universal way of life" and that Singapore by adopting it "might well become the seed of a future global culture looked to by other parts of the world".[12]

Even though Confucianism was only one of the six options in the Religious Knowledge curriculum, the sheer volume of discussion, consultation and other activities surrounding its introduction had tended to unnerve many among the non-Chinese. It was unfortunate that not many non-Chinese were willing to recognise that there was nothing exceptional and extraordinary about the special attention and publicity given to the teaching of Confucianism if one took into account the fact that the Chinese constituted some 77 per cent of the population of Singapore and that they alone among the different ethnic groups faced a serious threat to their heritage and traditional values. The problem seemed to be that by this time the Chinese had largely shed their general passiveness of the past and they had begun to assert themselves as the dominant majority. It was a new experience for the Malays and the Indians and naturally they took some time to adjust themselves to it.

Even though the Religious Knowledge curriculum was distinctly different from religious instruction, it created practical problems and unnecessary ethnic suspicion and controversy. Moreover, instead of promoting understanding of different religions among pupils and creating tolerance and harmony, it tended to accentuate one key basis of their separateness by reinforcing their commitment to their parents' religion. Obviously, the problem was, as with the government's earlier policy of bilingualism, that it was difficult to devise a Religious Knowledge curriculum that could serve two different, but equally important, purposes that it had in mind. One, to help pupils, the future citizens, to understand and adhere to the traditional values and precepts of their own community through a study of its religion; and two, to promote an understanding and tolerance of all the different religions in Singapore for the sake of ethnic peace and harmony. The Religious Knowledge curriculum that was introduced by the government included six different options and pupils were required to choose any one of them. The result was that it served only the first of the two above-mentioned purposes considered crucial by the government.

It was not surprising that in late 1989, the government took the decision to discontinue the teaching of religious knowledge as a compulsory subject and instead sought to widen and strengthen the existing, more general, civics or moral education programme to take its place. It was argued by Dr Tony Tan, the Minister of Education, that the responsibility for enhancing the religious knowledge of pupils had to rest primarily with their parents and that the state could only play a supporting role. According to a Singaporean academic studying public policy issues, in view of the worldwide trend of "a heightened consciousness of religious differences and a new fervour in the propagation of religious beliefs", it was extremely important that the government in Singapore adopted a "scrupulously neutral and evenhanded" approach to religious issues so that no strain was placed on religious tolerance and ethnic harmony.[13]

As a part of their overall objective to Asianise Singapore and restore the Chineseness of the Chinese, in 1980 the PAP government initiated the Special Assistance Plan (SAP) schools project. Initially, it provided for the conversion of nine Chinese secondary schools into special bilingual institutions that were to be especially funded by the government. The SAP schools were clearly intended to develop into prestigious élite schools as admission to them was restricted only to the top eight per cent of those passing the Primary School Leaving Examination. Despite the fact that these schools would prepare their students to be equally proficient in Mandarin and English, they were to have an essentially Chinese ambiance, in both linguistic and cultural terms. They would serve the following purposes:

1. To provide institutional facilities to enable top pupils, almost exclusively Chinese, to develop equal confidence in two languages, English and Mandarin, and be able to function with equal effectiveness in the two different worlds — western and Chinese — associated with them.
2. To preserve the traditional character and ethos of Chinese schools.
3. To assure the Chinese-speaking Singaporeans that the government was not indifferent to their concerns about the declining standards of competence in Mandarin.[14]

Recently, in January 1994, Prime Minister Goh Chok Tong, outlining the chief reason for establishing these schools, told this writer:

> The SAP schools were set up because we were concerned over the declining standard and use of Mandarin. We fear the disappearance of the Chinese cultural heritage and values if Singaporeans use only English. These schools are an attempt to preserve some very powerful assets of the Chinese community. They were not set up to allay the concerns of the Chinese-speaking with regard to their jobs or political position. No, the purpose is a larger one of preserving the important values and virtues of the Chinese community.
>
> ... In time to come, we hope that many of those at the top will be equally comfortable in English and Chinese, that is, be effectively bilingual. The SAP school students are amongst the brightest in the country. If the people at the top are proficient in Chinese and possess the strong virtues of the Chinese society, they will give Singapore its Asian ballast.[15]

It was not easy to argue that the introduction of SAP schools was of relevance and interest only to the Chinese community. It should not have surprised the PAP government that it caused some unease among the Malays and the Indians, and even amongst some English-educated Chinese. Their chief concerns were: firstly, that access to these prestigious, well-funded schools was restricted almost exclusively to Chinese students, for very few non-Chinese students were either to be in a position to meet the Mandarin language requirement or have the inclination to join a school with a strongly traditional Chinese environment; and secondly, that they were likely to deprive their Chinese students of the immensely valuable experience of mixing with students of other ethnic backgrounds at the most impressionable period of their lives. A senior Singapore educationist has shown further concern recently based on "the perception that these bright students are destined for future leadership positions in government, industry and other vital sectors and their enculturation in a 'Chinese' environment would limit their understanding of the values, expectations and norms of other communities."[16]

As we noted before, the problem of deculturisation was seen

by the government as a problem affecting chiefly the Chinese, and thus it believed that they alone needed special assistance to help them to recover and enhance their Chineseness. The government did not believe that the Malays and the Indians required any special assistance in this regard. The fact that the government did not, at the same time, provide for similar SAP schools for the Malays and the Indians has been viewed by some non-Chinese as discriminatory. Prime Minister Goh Chok Tong recently explained the situation to this writer:

> The government has to be even-handed. There had been suggestions by the Malays and Indians that the SAP schools were discriminatory as no such schools were established for them. So the answer is that if they want SAP schools for Malays and SAP schools for Indians, we can establish them. But the question is — is it in their interest? Do the Malays really need a SAP school to help preserve their culture and values when they are not being lost? We are prepared to establish SAP schools for them if they want them. But fortunately both communities have taken a practical view. They realise that if they were to have their own separate SAP schools in which Tamil or Malay is taught as the first language, they would be worse off. They do not have the numbers to make the SAP schools viable.[17]

Further to their attempt to Asianise Singapore and stem the tide of unwholesome western influences, during the late 1980s the PAP rulers set themselves to revitalise traditional Asian values. Their concern with regard to the decline in traditional Asian values was not a new one. The special attention given to the issue in the late 1980s seemed to have been reinforced by the publication of the influential study, *Ideology and National Competitiveness: An Analysis of Nine Countries*, by George C Lodge and Ezra F Vogel which obviously had been carefully studied by senior PAP leaders. New, more compelling reasons began to be canvassed by them for Asianising Singapore. They started to argue that if western individualistic tradition and attitudes were allowed to prevail over the traditional Asian communitarian commitments, in the future Singapore may find it increasingly difficult to sustain the high levels of economic achievements and prosperity attained by its populace during the past two decades. Singapore may also find it difficult to maintain the levels of social cohesion necessary for political stability and economic growth.

On 28 October 1988, in a speech to the PAP Youth Wing, First Deputy Prime Minister Goh Chok Tong (who had already been designated to succeed Prime Minister Lee Kuan Yew) first raised the notion of a national ideology, a set of core Asian values:

> Like Japan and Korea, Singapore is a high-performance country because we share the same cultural base as the other successful East Asians, that is, Confucian ethic. We have the same core values which made the Japanese, Koreans and Taiwanese succeed. If we want to continue to prosper we must not lose our core values such as hard work, thrift and sacrifice.
>
> The question is how to preserve them when daily we are exposed to alien influences. My suggestion is: formalise our values in a national ideology and then teach them in schools, workplaces, homes, as our way of life. Then we will have a set of principles to bind our people together and guide them forward.[18]

Only a few days before, addressing the Global Strategies Conference, Prime Minister Lee Kuan Yew had said that the East Asians "share many characteristics derived from a common cultural base, Chinese in origin. Some observers have attributed this emphasis on hard work and thrift to the 'Confucian ethic'".[19]

Within the Southeast Asian region, Indonesia had its national ideology in *Pancasila* and Malaysia in *Rukunegara*. The success of *Pancasila* in Indonesia in giving Indonesians a strong sense of unity and purpose had undoubtedly encouraged the PAP leaders to design a national ideology for Singapore. What they did not choose to take into account was the more relevant Malaysian experience with *Rukunegara*. *Pancasila* had been devised by President Sukarno during the Indonesian Revolution and therefore, a certain sanctity and mystique was attached to it. If Indonesians were to attempt to devise a national ideology today, they would find it to be a virtually impossible task. In Malaysia, which like Singapore possesses considerable ethnic diversity, *Rukunegara* was devised by a government that was entirely controlled by the Malays, during a period of extreme ethnic fear among the non-Malays resulting from the May 1969 riots and the government's handling of them. Thus *Rukunegara* had entirely failed in securing recognition by the non-Malays as a *national* ideology. It is extremely difficult to design a national ideology in multi-racial societies through the rational processes of discussion and debate. It is even more difficult to make it acquire a special sanctity and mystique, and emotionally move the country's diverse peoples.

During the following years, the issue of national ideology and core values (later, to ensure that no ethnic group felt left out, the government began to use the term *shared* values) was widely debated in Singapore. On 9 January 1989, in his address at the opening of the Seventh Parliament, President Wee Kim Wee identified the problem as viewed by the PAP government:

> Singapore is wide-open to external influences. Millions of foreign visitors pass through each year. Books, magazines, tapes and television programmes pour into Singapore every day. Most are from the developed countries of the West. The overwhelming bulk is in English. Because of universal English education, a new generation of Singaporeans absorbs their contents immediately, without translation or filtering.
>
> This openness has made us a cosmopolitan people, and put us in close touch with new ideas and technologies from abroad. But it has also exposed us to alien lifestyles and values. Under this pressure, in less than a generation, attitudes and outlooks of Singaporeans, especially younger Singaporeans, have shifted. Traditional Asian ideas of morality, duty and society which have sustained and guided us in the past are giving way to a more westernised, individualistic, and self-centred outlook on life.
>
> ... the speed and extent of the changes in Singapore society is worrying. We cannot tell what dangers lie ahead, as we rapidly grow more westernised.
>
> What sort of society will we become in another

generation? What sort of people do we want our children to become? Do we really want to abandon our own cultures and national identity? Can we build a nation of Singaporeans, in Southeast Asia, on the basis of values and concepts native to other peoples, living in other environments? How we answer these questions will determine our future.[20]

In his address, the President of Singapore then sought to set the national agenda on the issue:

> If we are not to lose our bearings, we should preserve the cultural heritage of each of our communities, and uphold certain common values which capture the essence of being a Singaporean. These core values include placing society above self, upholding the family as the basic block of society, resolving major issues through consensus instead of contention, and stressing racial and religious tolerance and harmony. We need to enshrine these fundamental ideas in a National Ideology. Such a formal statement will bond us together as Singaporeans, with our own distinct identity and destiny. We need to inculcate this National Ideology in all Singaporeans, especially the young.[21]

The government took special care to ensure that the National Ideology and Shared Values, like some of their other recent ideas and initiatives, were not seen to being overly based on the heritage and values of the Chinese. Views were sought from the representative organisations and leaders of the various ethnic segments. The choice of the specific values to be included, and their wording in broad general terms, was to facilitate their easy acceptance and adoption by the ethnic minorities. *In Search of Singapore's National Values*, published by the prestigious Institute of Policy Studies in mid-1990 to facilitate public discussion and debate on the issue, warned:

> Given the universal importance of the family, care must be taken when highlighting this core value to ensure that the government is not perceived by the minority groups to be

only promoting the Confucian model of the family as this will not be acceptable to the non-Chinese Singaporeans. It is quite easy to make the mistake of stressing Confucian family values only, especially when three-quarters of the population is of Chinese descent. The temptation to do so must be strenuously resisted . . . [22]

Even though this warning had related only to the core value of the importance of the family, it was equally applicable to all the other values constituting the National Ideology.

Brigadier-General Yeo, the Minister of State for Finance and a leading intellectual in the PAP, speaking at the National Ideology Forum for the Malay community, argued the need for a broader choice of ingredients to make up the National Ideology.[23] He insisted that Singapore must avoid "framing a narrow nationalism that cuts out the global outlook so essential to Singapore's economic development". It must combine the best of the East and the West. He warned: "If Chinese Singaporeans look only to Confucianism, the Malays and Indians will retreat into their own cultural and religious enclaves in self-defence, and all Singaporeans will be poorer off as a result."

A government White Paper on Shared Values issued in January 1991 especially sought to emphasise that Singapore was a multi-racial and multi-cultural society and that it had succeeded in the past in no small measure due to the distinctive cultures and value systems of its different communities. It acknowledged that the heritages of Singaporeans were diverse and that they could neither be reconciled totally with one another nor could they be "reduced to a single comprehensive doctrine". It suggested that Singapore's ethnic diversity instead of being allowed to act as a source of fragmentation should be utilised as a source of strength. It further said:

> We need to respect the great religions and cultures to which different groups of Singaporeans belong. Each religion or culture encompasses many enduring values, but unfortunately we cannot use any single one of them as the basis for building a common Singaporean identity, without alienating the other groups.[24]

It suggested that the way out of the dilemma was to identify "a few key values which are common to all the major groups in Singapore, and which draw on the essence of each of these heritages".[25] All communities would share these values

> ... although each will interpret and convey the same ideas in terms of their own cultural and religious traditions. The Malays will do so in Malay and Muslim terms, the Christians in terms of Bible stories and Christian traditions, many Chinese by reference to Confucian, Buddhist or Taoist teachings, the Hindus in terms of the Ramayana and Mahabharata, and so forth for other groups. This way, in time, all communities will gradually develop more common, distinctively Singaporean characteristics.[26]

In order to ensure that the different ethnic groups had no reason to have any strong reservations about the Shared Values, the government chose to modify and reword the four key values as outlined by the President of Singapore in his address to parliament in January 1989. Its White Paper of 6 January 1991 proposed that the following should form the basis for developing Shared Values among Singaporeans:

1. Nation before community and society above self.
2. Family as the basic unit of society.
3. Regard and community support for the individual.
4. Consensus instead of contention.
5. Racial and religious harmony.[27]

To allay the fears of the non-Chinese, the White Paper included a special section "Relationship with Confucianism". It acknowledged that initially non-Chinese Singaporeans had been concerned that the Shared Values might "become a subterfuge for imposing Chinese Confucian values on them". It sought to assure them that the PAP government had no intention of allowing the Chinese majority to impose its will on the minorities.[28] It emphasised:

> The Shared Values must be shared by all communities. Confucian Ethics cannot be so shared. But the Chinese

community can draw upon Confucian concepts which form part of their heritage, to elaborate the abstract Shared Values into concrete examples and vivid stories.

Many Confucian ideals are relevant to Singapore. For example, the importance of human relationships and of placing society above self are key ideas in the Shared Values. The concept of government by honourable men, *junzi*, who have a duty to do right for the people, and who have the trust and respect of the population, fits us better than the western idea that a government should be given as limited powers as possible, and should always be treated with suspicion unless proven otherwise.

But even for Chinese Singaporeans the Shared Values cannot just be Confucianism by another name. Precepts and practices which evolved in a rural, agricultural society have to be revised to fit an urban, industrial society. Confucianism has no monopoly of virtue. It needs to be brought up-to-date and reconciled with other ideas which are also essential parts of our ethos.[29]

For some time, the attempt to design a National Ideology was taken very seriously by the Singapore government; it even sought to learn from the experience of Indonesia. The Singapore government had concluded in its White Paper on Shared Values that the major concern of the different communities — that the shared values must be compatible with their own specific beliefs and practices — had been met. Eventually, however, it found it extremely difficult to design a National Ideology which was not heavily based on Confucian ethic, included values common to all ethnic segments and at the same time served the critical purpose of providing strong national underpinnings for continuing economic expansion and growth and Singapore's political and ethnic stability. The countries which had constituted the models of remarkable progress were the East Asian countries of Japan, Korea and Taiwan which, in the words of Prime Minister Lee Kuan Yew, had "a common cultural base, Chinese in origin" and was derived from Confucian ethic. In his address to the PAP Youth Wing in October 1988, when he had first formally suggested the need to have a National Ideology, Goh Chok Tong, then First Deputy Prime Minister, said:

> I have just started on a book by the two Harvard professors, George Lodge and Ezra Vogel [Vogel also wrote *Japan as Number One*]. It is called *Ideology and National Competitiveness*. Their thesis is this: the national competitiveness of a country is affected by whether its people are more "communitarian" or "individualistic". Every society has both these elements, but each differs in the dominance of one over the other. In Japan, Korea and Taiwan, communitarianism dominates individualism. This has allowed them to catch up economically with the industrial West in the last 20 years. Japan, because of its communitarian value, is unbeatable, according to Ezra Vogel.[30]

Obviously, the communitarianism that had worked in the case of Japan, Korea and Taiwan was Chinese communitarianism based on Confucian ethic. But the Singaporean Malays were rooted in a distinctively different communitarianism of their own, which they shared with the Indonesians and the Malaysian Malays, but that communitarianism has not been spectacularly successful in constituting the basis of economic achievements in those countries. In fact, for long it had been viewed by many as the major obstacle in the way of Malay and Indonesian progress and achievements. So, the unavoidable truth was that what Singapore really needed in order to maintain continuing economic progress and prosperity, and political stability was the restoration essentially of the vigour of Chinese communitarianism. In any case, the need for the initiative had arisen in the first place only because the hold on the Singaporean Chinese and their traditional values and Confucian ethic, associated with communitarianism, had eroded considerably. Not surprisingly, it did not take long before the attempt by the government to design a National Ideology was given up.

However, despite the fact that certain initiatives of the PAP rulers had not worked out, the dramatic shift in the application of their founding principle of a multi-racial cultural democracy that they had initiated in 1979 remained non-reversible. Their new agenda for Asianising Singapore, including restoring the Chineseness of the Chinese, continued to be pursued with undiminished vigour. Government leaders began to make special exhortations to Singaporeans to learn their own mother tongues, retain their distinctive heritages and traditional values, and revitalise their cultural moorings. Through a variety of government policies and actions, the message to Singaporeans was clear throughout that the government placed very high priority on Asianising Singapore. The Ministries of Community Development and Information and the Arts made special efforts to get the different ethnic segments to organise activities geared to preserving their distinctive identities, languages and cultures. The result was an unprecedented display of the cultural variety represented by the different peoples of Singapore. Cultural groups and clubs were formed by the different communities at the various Community Centres scattered all over Singapore. Encouraged and assisted by the government, communities began to organise their own special cultural months. They began to organise certain traditional religious ceremonies and cultural performances now with an enhanced zeal and a new and undisguised sense of pride.

With the start of this second phase, concerned chiefly with Asianising Singapore, the ethnic environment in Singapore had also begun to change markedly. In the past, since independence, the first-generation PAP rulers had placed severe limitations on free discussion and debate of sensitive ethnic issues by Singaporeans, including politicians and the mass media, fearing that it could easily damage ethnic relationships and create confrontation and conflict. Manifestations of ethnic extremism were crushed mercilessly. Persons, political parties and media organisations stepping out of the bounds of these limitations were punished severely by the tough, no-nonsense first-generation rulers. Fear of the government had been so extreme that few had ever dared to step out of line. Although there was little public airing of ethnic problems, fears and prejudices, it was an unprecedented era of ethnic peace and quiet.

By the beginning of the decade of the 1980s, the situation had begun to change significantly. A new, second generation of PAP leaders, who had little personal experience of the ethnic as well as the ideological battles of the 1950s and the early 1960s, had come to the forefront and had begun to assume increasing responsibilities for governing Singapore. They had gone through higher education and grown to adulthood during the post-independence period when Singapore had seen few manifestations of ethnic disharmony and conflict. The integrative policies of the PAP and its agenda of creating an essentially English-speaking Singapore had a marked effect on their ethnic persona and their relationships with persons from other ethnic backgrounds. Essentially, they represented the first generation of real Singaporeans.

The second-generation PAP leaders had come to believe, based on their own experience and perspective, that Singaporeans, representing different ethnic segments, had attained such a level of maturity and a sense of ethnic responsibility that they could handle candid public discussion of ethnic issues and problems without necessarily precipitating ethnic disharmony and conflict. They had also felt that much of the ethnic extremism of the pre-independence days had dissipated itself and there were few political leaders and organisations left in Singapore that could take advantage of open debate and discussion of ethnic issues for their own dysfunctional purposes. Thus the second-generation PAP leaders were more willing to take the lead and seek to face more forthrightly issues and problems involving acute ethnic sensitivities.

One of the most important areas of their concern in this regard was the problem of the growing disparities between ethnic segments as well as within the Chinese community, between the English-speaking and the Chinese-speaking. It was not that in the past the first-generation PAP rulers had failed to concern themselves at all with the issue. Their attitude then had been chiefly guided by the notion that so long as there was continuing economic growth and prosperity, which allowed Singaporeans adequate opportunities for employment and personal advancement, they did not need to worry especially about the impact of disparities on ethnic relationships and the overall ethnic environment in Singapore.

At the time of independence in 1965, Singapore was not vastly different from other Third World states. An overwhelming majority of its people were poor, enjoying low standards of health, housing and education. Unemployment was commonplace among them. Because of the reality of their deprivation and poverty during the period of British rule, to the ordinary Singaporeans the economic progress and prosperity achieved by the PAP government during the 1970s had undoubtedly been spectacular. It gave them a good feeling that jobs were more easily available and increasing numbers of them were able to own cheap subsidised Housing Development Board flats, better than any they had lived in before; ownership of HDB flats had given them a specially heightened sense of pride and satisfaction. Their children were able to go to continually improving schools and they had access to greatly improved health services. All this, during the 1970s, had produced a high level of satisfaction among most Singaporeans and this was reflected throughout the period in their voting behaviour. Not many of them, especially the Chinese, were disposed to worrying about the growing disparities of incomes and wealth between Singaporeans as well as between ethnic segments. On the whole, there seemed little reason for Prime Minister Lee Kuan Yew and his colleagues to seriously worry if the existing disparities would strain ethnic relationships and cause confrontation and conflict between different groups.

Starting from about 1980, coinciding with their new special agenda of Asianising Singapore, the PAP rulers began to show some concern about the growing disparities between ethnic segments, but for about a decade, until the transfer of power to PAP's second-generation leaders in 1990, their concern had remained restricted almost entirely to the position of the indigenous Malays. They believed that the problem of disparities in respect of the others could easily be exaggerated. A preeminent second-generation leader of the PAP told this writer in mid-1983:

> Inequalities in reality are not very substantial. Their level within a very large part of the population, some 70 per cent, is extremely limited. This constitutes the large group of people whose incomes range from S$300 to S$800. The

difference within this group between the highest and the lowest is not that great. It is only the small number of people outside this group who earn very high incomes. But their numbers are so small that the disparity does not matter much. Moreover, they occupy key positions and without them the economic progress would have been difficult to achieve. If they were not paid such high salaries, they would tend to leave Singapore. The 70 per cent on lower incomes then would inevitably suffer.[31]

The English-educated Chinese had benefited the most from Singapore's spectacular economic expansion and growth of the 1970s. They had come to enjoy vast new opportunities for advancement which, it was believed, would keep them occupied and make them desist from any dysfunctional activity prejudicial to ethnic peace and harmony. In any case, the English-educated had come to constitute the new rulers of Singapore. Even though they had been full of resentment against what they had perceived as discrimination against them by the English-educated rulers of Singapore ever since independence, the Chinese-educated had then possessed neither the leadership nor the courage to give expression to their feelings publicly. It was essentially starting from the late 1980s, when power had begun to be assumed by the second-generation PAP leaders, that the disparity between them and the English-educated Chinese, in terms of both economic and political power, became a contentious issue. As for the Indians, the extremely small size of their population had made it virtually impossible for them to be able to influence, damagingly or otherwise, the overall environment of ethnic relationships in Singapore substantially. Furthermore, a significantly large group of well-educated Indians occupied senior positions in a variety of professions and public services, which gave the rank and file of the Indian community a certain sense of pride, participation and powerfulness.

As a result, the PAP rulers' initial worries with regard to disparities related only to the indigenous Malays. The fear was that the Malays had not been able to take advantage of the opportunities, even those that were specifically made available to them as the *bumiputra*, and that the gap between them and the others, especially the Chinese, continued to widen and eventually in the future was likely to create a serious problem of ethnic management. Even in their case, this was not seen by the PAP rulers as an immediate, urgent problem. Essentially, they believed that time was on the side of the government and that what was needed immediately was only a form of assistance to the Malays that made it possible for them to improve their position in relation to the others. Asked if the government had been concerned about the growing disparity between the Malays and the Chinese, a pre-eminent second-generation leader of the PAP told this writer in mid-1983:

> We have fears about it but there is little we can do beyond giving the Malays special help in certain respects. Undoubtedly, Singapore Malays have changed to a degree. They are able to acquire certain skills, become technicians. In the universities, however, the Malays, who have been doing well and then going on into professions or higher levels of the public service, have tended to be only part-Malay. Many of them are part-Indian or part-Arab.[32]

Mindful of the especially strong sensitivities of the Malays, at this time the PAP rulers were not willing to go beyond the problems of education and skills in focusing the attention of the Malay community and offering it special assistance in its attempts to deal with them. The number of Malays who had graduated from university in the previous six years, had ranged from 22 in 1976 to 27 in 1981. They represented a tiny proportion of their generation of about 8,000 in 1976 and 10,000 in 1981, who had started primary schooling in the same year. On the whole, the performance of Malay students in the English language courses had not been very good and this had been making it more difficult for them than other Singaporeans to progress to higher levels of education. To rectify the situation, the government believed that a community-run programme was to achieve the greatest success as, in the words of Prime Minister Lee Kuan Yew, the community "will be more effective with Malay/Muslim parents than the government school teachers and principals. You can reach them through their hearts, not simply their minds".[33]

It wanted the programme to be based on the notion of self-help rather than dependence on government action and handouts.

As a result, in 1981 a large number of Malay organisations in Singapore, encouraged by the PAP government, formed MENDAKI (Council on Education for Malay/Muslim Children) as a joint body with the objective "to improve the level of educational achievement by Malay/Muslim students, and to increase the number and percentage of higher-educated Malays/Muslims".[34] Even though MENDAKI depended both on the Malay community as well as the government for its finances, for obvious reasons it sought to emphasise its dependence on the community. Community support came through voluntary donations, in most cases $1 per month paid through the government's Central Provident Fund by most Muslim wage earners. The government contributed an amount equal to the total of annual voluntary donations by Malays/Muslims, subject to a stipulated maximum. The government also provided staff and suitable accommodation to MENDAKI.

Despite the fact that the PAP rulers launched the Speak Mandarin Campaign in 1979 to encourage the Chinese to make greater use of Mandarin, they showed no special reluctance in taking an entirely practical view on the highly emotional issue of language and publicly urging Malay children to use more English than their mother tongue, Malay. They did not worry about the fact that the Malays could easily misconstrue their exhortation and charge that instead of promoting and enhancing the use of Malay language (as they were doing for the Chinese through their Speak Mandarin Campaign), a core component of their Malayness, they were attempting to dilute their Malayness by asking them to make their children use more English. The government's idea had been based on a study of the correlation between home language and mean score at Primary School Leaving Examination which had demonstrated that the more English was used by pupils at home, the better their performance had been. Prime Minister Lee Kuan Yew, in his address at the opening of the MENDAKI Congress on 28 May 1982, had sought to candidly spell out the situation to the Malay community:

Language is the key to acquisition of knowledge. If a student is unable to understand a language, then he is unable to receive information or knowledge in that language. It is therefore crucial that a breakthrough must be made in the English language and as early in life as possible. From the 1980 Census, Singapore Malays, more than Chinese, Indians or others, invariably used their mother tongue, Malay, at home. In other words, apart from school or office or workplace, their language is Malay.

Parents have to decide on the trade-off between the convenience of speaking Malay or the mother tongue at home with their children at the cost of EL1 (English Language 1). If they want their children to do well in EL1, their children must also speak English at home; if not to the parents, then to brothers, sisters and neighbours.[35]

MENDAKI performed quite well during the following years. In 1982, it had started with six centres, offering special tuition by professionally qualified teachers, and 880 students.[36] Seven years later, in 1989, when it held its second congress, it had sixteen tuition centres catering to the needs of 4,450 students. The overall performance of Malay students during the period too had begun to improve markedly. For example, in 1980 only sixteen per cent of Malay students obtained at least five 'O' level results, but by 1988 the figure had risen to 42 per cent. On the whole, based on the work and achievements of MENDAKI, by 1989 the PAP government had come to have a more optimistic view of the Malays being able to make further progress and narrow the gap between them and the others.

This was the time when, for all practical purposes, Singapore had begun to be governed by the second-generation PAP leaders headed by Deputy Prime Minister Goh Chok Tong, who had come to be seen by the Malays as having a more sympathetic and constructive view of them and their aspirations. As we shall see later in the following chapter, Deputy Prime Minister Goh Chok Tong and his second-generation colleagues became far more concerned about the problem of disparity between ethnic segments and the position of the underclass in Singapore than the first-generation leaders. Reflecting that concern and not overly worrying about Malay sensitivities, Deputy Prime Minister Goh Chok Tong, in his speech to MENDAKI's second congress on 19 May 1989, publicly called upon Malay community leaders to work for more wide-ranging social change among their people by dealing with a variety of other problems that stood in the way of their achieving greater progress:

> To uplift the Malay community you will have to adopt a total approach. It cannot be through education alone, important and basic though this is. For example, there are those who have already left school. They need to be helped to raise their standard of living. There are special problem areas, like youths going astray and ending up wasting their lives away as drug addicts.[37]

Deputy Prime Minister Goh identified the following major social problems that needed to be addressed by the Malay community: low incomes, drug abuse, an increasing number of cases of divorce, single parents and poor parenting. These were problems that chiefly afflicted the Malay underclass, which constituted a significantly large proportion of their community. He was especially concerned about this large group and considered it essential that its position was improved. Noting that little work had been done to study the problems of the Malay underclass, he suggested that, to start with, MENDAKI should set up a research and survey unit and for this purpose he offered it an initial sum of $250,000 per year.

Clearly, the second-generation leaders considered the implications of the problems faced by the indigenous Malays as so serious that they were not willing to continue to show the traditional regard for Malay feelings and let the problems be treated as entirely an internal affair of the community. They were conscious that the problems related to issues of such extreme sensitivity that any comment or advice from the government could easily be strongly resented by the Malays and be branded as an entirely uncalled-for interference in their society and its affairs. The Indian community too had a large underclass that faced serious social problems, but in their case the government had chosen not to involve itself at all; it had followed the general attitude of treating the Indian underclass as an internal affair of the community. Despite the danger of a hostile reaction of sections within the Malay community, Deputy Prime Minister Goh and his second-generation colleagues were determined to push the community into dealing with a variety of problems facing it.

As the process of Asianising Singapore gained momentum, the country came to have an increasingly more open ethnic environment. In this regard, the lead had been taken by the PAP rulers who publicly began to reflect on ethnic issues with unprecedented openness and candour. This new approach had been welcomed among the Chinese, but on certain issues it created considerable concern among the Malays and the Indians. For example, just before the 1988 general elections, Brigadier-General Lee Hsien Loong had chosen to discuss publicly the issue of the exclusion of the Malays from the Singapore air force, navy and certain sections of the army. The policy had been well known in the past, but it had remained unstated and unpublicised. It had been accepted by the Malays and it had not seemed to cause any special anger among them; on the whole, they had tended to understand it. But according to a Malay leader of the PAP, once the policy had been publicly argued and defended

> . . . the Malays had to face the awkward position in the open that their government had no faith in their loyalty to Singapore and that it did not want to take the risk of jeopardising the security of the country by allowing Malays into the services.[38]

The new openness of the PAP leaders was easily emulated by the different peoples of Singapore and their community leaders. Ethnic issues and problems, which in the past had never been allowed to be publicly aired, now began to be openly discussed and reported in the mass media, often encouraged by the PAP leaders themselves. The fear of government retribution among Singaporeans in this regard diminished considerably. The result was a general blooming of the proverbial "hundred flowers", and the different ethnic segments began to express themselves openly and make demands on behalf of their peoples. The resurgence among the Chinese, based on their position as the dominant majority, was that much greater and noisier. They were able to shed their excessively cautious attitude of the past and openly began to espouse the cause of their identity, language and culture.

This dramatically changing ethnic environment and the PAP government's policies aimed at Asianising Singapore, including restoring the Chineseness of the Chinese, had created considerable dissatisfaction and concern among the Malays. The central problem was that the initiatives of the PAP government since 1979 that had been geared to Asianising Singapore, beginning with the Speak Mandarin Campaign, had come to be increasingly viewed by the Malays (as well as by the Indians) as constituting a shift from the founding principle of a multi-racial cultural democracy and representing a possible move towards the Sinicisation of Singapore. A pre-eminent Malay leader of the PAP told this writer in December 1988 that the Malays had begun to resent the strong reassertion of Chineseness in Singapore by the Chinese as well as the government. To them, it had been reflected in the emphasis on Mandarin and the Speak Mandarin Campaign, the attempt to excessively promote Confucianism for some time and the little things like the naming of new roads and new townships. The Malays viewed this as a deviation from the concept of multi-racialism as devised and introduced in the 1960s. According to him, they suspected that the old commitment of the PAP to de-emphasise the Chineseness of Singapore had begun to erode.

> When Singapore was forced out of Malaysia in 1965, its PAP leaders had to set up a genuinely multi-racial Singapore, a Singapore that was acceptable to its Malay neighbours. They had established a polity which at least formally recognised all the different racial groups as equal, enjoying the same rights and status; they could not have then allowed the Chinese a pre-eminent position and their language and culture a special status.
>
> The second-generation leaders of the government and the Singapore Chinese, in general, today are no more

strongly influenced by the imperatives of the sixties. With the impressive economic growth and prosperity of the past two decades, the Chinese have gained a new confidence. They do not have any more worries about the viability of an independent Singapore. They are the dominant majority and they want to act that part now. And to many Malays, the PAP government seems to be more interested in appeasing the Chinese in order to maintain their large electoral support than strictly upholding the principle of multi-racialism that in 1965 had guaranteed an equality of rights and status to all the different communities.[39]

Such Malay feelings were reflected in the change in their voting behaviour in the 1988 general elections. Apparently a significant number of Malays had chosen not to vote for the PAP candidates. The PAP rulers had then taken a serious and angry view of the Malays' voting behaviour. Some of the criticism heaped on the Malay community by them had a certain tone of impatience. Deputy Prime Minister Goh Chok Tong, who had already been showing greater concern for the problems faced by the Malays, had been especially disappointed. While addressing the Malay/Muslim Development Congress on 19 May 1989, he frankly told the leaders of the Malay community that he wanted a clear commitment by a majority of Malays to the government that they genuinely wanted it to work with them to achieve the aspirations of their community. He said that he was puzzled that even though they wanted the government to do more for the Malay community, they did not come out openly to support it. On the whole, there was little doubt that the government's various initiatives since 1979 aimed at Asianising Singapore, had put a strain on its relationship with the indigenous Malays. Many Malays had begun to lose their confidence in the PAP rulers. Some had even begun to doubt if the new, second-generation PAP rulers could have the same depth of commitment to the Malays and to multi-racialism as the first-generation PAP rulers. The latter had governed during a period when Indonesian Confrontation and the two years of constant controversy and conflict within Malaysia, based largely upon their quest for a Malaysian Malaysia, had sensitised them fully to the critical compulsions of governing a predominantly Chinese Singapore based in the middle of the Malay world of Southeast Asia.

However, the problem involved in the PAP rulers' attempts to Asianise Singapore was a critical one and related not only to the Malays. Throughout this second phase of their management of ethnic diversity, the PAP rulers had faced extreme difficulty in tailoring their various initiatives aimed at Asianising Singapore to fully reflect Singapore's ethnic diversity and and not to be seen to be excessively based upon the Chinese community and its distinctive language, heritage and values. The problem had largely been created by the fact that during the period 1965 to 1979, the PAP rulers' policies to create an essentially English-speaking Singapore had their greatest impact on the Chinese, in the increasing erosion of their commitment to their cultural heritage and traditional values, and thus it was essentially they whose Asianness needed to be restored and enhanced. The Malays had come through that era of intense social engineering essentially escaping any significant erosion in their commitment to their Malay/Muslim way of life and values; and the same was largely true of the small population of Indians. Inevitably, therefore, the PAP rulers' initiatives aimed at Asianising Singapore had to be chosen especially to obtain the maximum change among the Chinese and, in their implementation, to be targeted especially at the Chinese; in effect, seeking the enhancement of their Chineseness. Furthermore, as the Chinese constituted a large majority of the population, it was only natural that the level of cultural and linguistic activity relating to the initiatives among them was far greater and on a scale much grander (in view of the vastly superior financial and other resources available to them) than among the Malays and the Indians. But unfortunately, it tended to be unnerving for the Malays and the Indians, often creating fears among them that Singapore may be becoming more Chinese.

As we shall see in the following chapter, after the transfer of power to them in 1990, the second-generation PAP rulers have been seeking to reassure the Malays and the Indians that a multi-racial cultural democracy remains the founding principle of Singapore. Beyond that they have been developing new dimensions of the rationale for their overall agenda of Asianising Singapore which are likely to make it more meaningful to the Malays and the Indians and possibly even dispel their fears of any erosion in the government's continuing commitment to the founding principle of a multi-racial cultural democracy as devised by the first-generation rulers of Singapore.

Notes

1 Interview with a PAP leader, Singapore, September 1993.
2 S Gopinathan, "Language Policy Changes, 1979–92: Politics and Pedagogy", unpublished paper, 1993, p. 4.
3 Quoted in Tham Song Chee, "The Perception and Practice of Education", in K S Sandhu and Paul Wheatley (editors), *Management of Success: The Moulding of Modern Singapore*, Singapore 1993, p. 486.
4 Committee to Promote the Use of Mandarin, Government of Singapore, *Speak Mandarin Campaign Launching Speeches, 1979–89*, p. 10.
5 *Ibid.*, p. 40.
6 *Ibid.*, p. 40.
7 *Ibid.*, pp. 39–40.
8 Jon S T Quah, "Government Policies and National Building", in Jon S T Quah (editor), *In Search of Singapore's National Values*, Institute of Policy Studies, Singapore 1990, p. 57.
9 Committee to Promote the Use of Mandarin, Government of Singapore, *Speak Mandarin Campaign Launching Speeches, 1978–89*, p. 72.
10 Trevor Ling, "Religion", in K S Sandhu and Paul Wheatley (editors), *Management of Success: The Moulding of Modern Singapore*, Singapore 1993, p. 702.
11 *Ibid.*, p. 702.
12 *Ibid.*, p. 702.
13 Jon S T Quah, "Government Policies and National Building", in Jon S T Quah (editor), *In Search of Singapore's National Values*, Institute of Policy Studies, Singapore 1990, p. 55.
14 S Gopinathan, "Language Policy Changes, 1979–1992: Politics and Pedagogy", unpublished paper, p. 6.
15 Interview with Goh Chok Tong, Singapore, January 1994.
16 S Gopinathan, "Language Policy Changes, 1979–1992: Politics and Pedagogy", unpublished paper, p. 6.
17 Interview with Goh Chok Tong, Singapore, January 1994.
18 Ministry of Communications and Information, *Speeches, A Bimonthly Selection of Ministerial Speeches*, Singapore, September–October 1988, p. 15.
19 Quoted in *ibid.*, p. 14.

20 *Shared Values*, Government of Singapore, White Paper, 6 January 1991, p. 1.
21 *Ibid.*, pp. 1–2.
22 Jon S T Quah, *In Search of Singapore's National Values*, Institute of Policy Studies, Singapore 1990, p. 94.
23 *The Straits Times*, 18 December 1988.
24 *Shared values*, Government of Singapore, White Paper, 6 January 1991, p. 3.
25 *Ibid.*, p. 3.
26 *Ibid.*, p. 3.
27 *Ibid.*, p. 3.
28 *Ibid.*, p. 7.
29 *Ibid.*, p. 8.
30 Goh Chok Tong, First Deputy Prime Minister, "Our National Ethic", in Ministry of Communications and Information, *Speeches, A Bimonthly Selection of Ministerial Speeches*, Singapore, September–October 1988.
31 Interview with a pre-eminent second-generation leader of the PAP, Singapore, mid-1983.
32 *Ibid.*
33 Prime Minister Lee Kuan Yew, address at the opening of the Congress of MENDAKI (the Council on Education for Muslim Children) on 28 May 1982, in *Making the Difference: Ten Years of MENDAKI*, Singapore 1989, p. 17.
34 Speech by Dr Ahmad Mattar, Acting Minister of Community Affairs and Chairman of MENDAKI, at the opening of the Congress of MENDAKI, 28 May 1982, *ibid.*, p. 18.
35 *Ibid.*, p. 17.
36 *Ibid.*, p. 19.
37 *Ibid.*, p. 20.
38 Interview with a pre-eminent Malay leader of the PAP, Singapore, December 1988.
39 Interview with a pre-eminent Malay leader of the PAP, Singapore, December 1988.

CHAPTER 6

Management of Ethnicity: Since 1990

On 28 November 1990, Goh Chok Tong, representing the second-generation leadership, took over as Prime Minister of Singapore from Lee Kuan Yew who had held that position for more than three decades. This generational change of leadership, even though it had signified the end of an era, did not mean a drastic departure from the approach and policies adopted by the first-generation rulers relating to management of Singapore's ethnic diversity. The hallmark of Prime Minister Goh Chok Tong's new government had to be continuity and change.

The second-generation leaders had been carefully chosen by the first-generation founding fathers of Singapore over a long period of time. The former had long been associated with the PAP government, much of them serving as apprentices under training by Prime Minister Lee Kuan Yew and his close associates. Their personalities and outlook, as well as their view of the policies needed to secure and enhance the interests of Singapore and its people, had been substantially moulded by their chief tutor and mentor, Lee Kuan Yew. Throughout the period they had been members of the government and had no notable disagreements with the first-generation leaders with regard to the fundamentals of government policy and action. Prime Minister Goh Chok Tong and his colleagues in the new government had the greatest respect for Lee Kuan Yew and his first-generation colleagues as the creators of modern Singapore. They were in awe of their intellect, their management skills and their record of achievements in all facets of Singapore's existence. They recognised that the policies initiated by the founding fathers had been the best-suited to the enhancement of ethnic harmony and social and economic progress. It was not just sentiment and a concession to Asian values that had made Prime Minister Goh Chok Tong ask Lee Kuan Yew to remain in the new government and occupy a special position as Senior Minister. There was, therefore, no question of the new government seeking to change course and initiating a new set of fundamental policies.

With regard to the critical issue of management of Singapore's extreme ethnic diversity, Prime Minister Goh Chok Tong and his new government were to maintain continuity. They were to retain their overall commitment to the founding principle of a multi-racial cultural democracy.

However, in developing their own approach to the actual management of ethnicity Prime Minister Goh Chok Tong and his second-generation colleagues could not ignore the fact that the key factors that had influenced the thinking and policies of the first-generation rulers for some two decades had changed markedly. By the late 1980s, the geo-political environment in the region had improved so much that Singaporeans could now live their lives without having to worry continually and excessively about the survival of the immensely prosperous Singapore they had built. Their new government could now govern the island and pursue policies, domestic as well as international, promoting the interests of its peoples without having to take into account too much the views and sensibilities of its powerful neighbours. Singapore had come to be fully accepted as a member of the ASEAN family of nations and its government had developed close relations with its neighbours, Malaysia and Indonesia, based upon mutuality of advantage. The Singapore government had come to find itself in a position where it could deal with controversial and sensitive internal ethnic issues forthrightly and far more directly.

Furthermore, there had been the remarkable transformation of the social and economic reality of Singapore during the past two decades thanks to the spectacular progress and prosperity achieved under PAP rule. Equally significant had been the changes in the ethnic environment and relationships resulting from the success of the government's efforts during the preceding ten years or so to Asianise Singapore.

Firstly, with better education, full employment and vastly improved standards of living and access to mass media, more and more Singaporeans had begun to demand of their rulers that they be treated as citizens of a democracy. They believed that the time had come when the government should not only be satisfying the Confucian precept of working for the well-being and prosperity of Singaporeans, but also that it should make itself more directly accountable to them and more responsive to their wishes. It should be consulting them and allowing them meaningful participation in the governance of their country. Since the Chinese account for more than three-quarters of Singapore's population, Prime Minister Goh Chok Tong and his government thus had little choice but to start giving more attention to the voices and stirrings in that community. The declining Malay electoral support for the PAP, which had first come to notice in the 1984 general elections, had tended to give additional impetus to this imperative.

Prime Minister Goh Chok Tong and his second-generation colleagues had begun to become more conscious of these changing attitudes of Singaporeans from the early 1980s when they had been allowed by the first-generation rulers to assume greater responsibility for governing Singapore as their successors. Talking about the future when they would have assumed power, a top-ranking second-generation leader told this writer in 1983 that

> ... in the initial years, five to seven years, we would have to make a very strong effort to ensure much greater consultation with the people. We would have to be seen to be talking with them, consulting them. This would be one major change when the second generation takes over.[1]

From the beginning, Goh Chok Tong as Prime Minister indeed sought to give his government a new, gentler, non-combative image by adopting a consultative and a more open political style.

The inevitable result has been that since their accession to power in 1990, Singapore has become a markedly more open and free society. Singaporeans and their media have begun to show far less fear of their government. Many of them have been greatly more willing to give expression to their views than ever before.

Secondly, the government's special attempts since the late 1970s to Asianise Singapore, entailing encouragement and assistance to the different communities to maintain and enhance their distinctive languages and cultures, created a new sense of extreme pride in the ethnic identities of all the different peoples, including the Chinese. Not many in the general public, except possibly a few Indians, any longer showed a special interest in the introduction of new, more directly integrative policies by the government that brought about further blurring of the ethnic differences and created a common, distinctive Singaporean identity and way of life. On this issue, even the essentially lone prominent voice of one of the founding fathers of modern Singapore, S Rajaratnam, mostly tended to fail to attract much public attention and support. Recently, a top-ranking leader of the government, when asked if there were many in Singapore who sought ethnic integration, asserted to this writer:

> Not many people think of ethnic integration in Singapore. The Chinese want to remain Chinese, the Malays want to remain Malay and the Indians want to remain Indian. Who are the people in Singapore who want to be integrated, and into what? So in Singapore, the issue is not that of integration. The real question is how Singaporeans can be made to retain their distinctive identities, cultures and heritages as equals and showing understanding of each other.[2]

The present PAP rulers rarely exhort Singaporeans to develop and subscribe especially to a new common Singaporean identity. They are not using any of their exceptional intellectual and technocratic talents to design any new initiatives of their own in this regard. The PAP rulers are determined to concentrate their efforts on Asianising Singapore. They are satisfied that the variety of integrative policies — relating to education, public housing, maintenance of a friction-free ethnic environment and general economic modernisation and advancement — that had been introduced by the first-generation rulers should continue to maintain the necessary minimum level of ethnic understanding and intermingling. Their calculations in respect of their management of ethnicity in the future are based upon a Singaporean reality in which they expect increasingly to deal with three distinct communities — the Chinese, the Malays and the Indians — each proud of its own ethnicity, not fearful any more of losing its identity and enjoying a recognised, special place of its own in a thriving, multi-racial and tolerant Singapore.

The cumulative result of these has been that the government, under the influence of the second-generation leaders, has allowed an unprecedented manifestation of ethnicity and a new ethnic openness since the late 1980s. For about a quarter century, while Singapore was ruled by the first-generation leaders, ethnic issues and relationships had been strictly excluded from public discussion and debate. Breaches of the restriction carried such extreme penalties that few amongst the public or the media had ever dared to step out of line. But now there is open, considerably uninhibited public discussion of sensitive ethnic issues, often initiated by leaders of the government themselves, including Senior Minister Lee Kuan Yew, who consider their forthrightness and plain-speaking on the issues to be a special virtue: "We now try to discuss outstanding problems and ethnic issues openly. It is better than what was done before because it helps us in dealing with ethnic issues and resolving the problems".[3]

It has also meant that the different communities, starting from the late 1980s, have shown far less inhibition than before in making demands publicly in respect of their languages and cultures, their political role and status, and the economic lot of their members. In the absence of any extreme fear of Prime Minister Goh Chok Tong's government, community leaders and PAP members of parliament have begun to speak publicly on behalf of their communities. In the past, the first-generation rulers, fearful of ethnic controversy and conflict, strictly controlled public airing of ethnic aspirations and complaints. These were either discussed internally within the communities or "negotiated" informally by their leaders with the government, mostly out of public view.

Among the Chinese, the patience and lack of assertiveness they displayed for more than two decades, based upon a general fear about their future within Singapore as well as the larger world of Southeast Asia, has started becoming a thing of the past. Most Chinese now are Singapore-born and Singapore is the only home to them. They are Singaporeans and it is *their* Singapore and they, along with other Singaporeans, must determine its destiny. There have been clear signs of a certain restiveness among sections of the Chinese who have been dissatisfied with the absence of any special, visible recognition of their community's status as the dominant majority. Increasing numbers of young Chinese, even those from westernised, English-educated families, have been rediscovering their Chineseness and are taking full pride in it. The economic miracle of Singapore, giving them a personal life of affluence and plenty, has given them a new sense of powerfulness. This makes it much more difficult for them to appreciate fully the compulsions, ethnic as well as geo-political, that had guided the first-generation PAP rulers in devising their strategy for the management of ethnicity, which included de-emphasising the Chineseness of Singapore as a critical element.

A new Chinese leadership, mostly bilingual (primarily Chinese-speaking but being able to handle English with considerable ease) and still strongly rooted within the community, has emerged that has been extremely vocal in making demands about the position of the Chinese, their language and culture. They enjoy strong backing from their traditional community leaders as well as from the extremely influential Chinese language newspapers. Most of them are closely associated with the PAP; some of them even hold important positions within the party or the government. They have been well represented in the parliament. The prominent and the more visible ones among them have been Ong Teng Cheong, a top-ranking second-generation leader who had held several senior cabinet positions and was elected to the position of the President of Singapore in 1993, and Dr Ow Chin Hock, who was a senior economist at the National University of Singapore until recently and is now the chief executive of a private company. Unlike their predecessors of the 1950s and the 1960s, they have not been tainted by their being communists, being the agents of the old Malayan Communist Party. In the new environment in which the government itself is determined to Asianise Singapore and restore the Chineseness of the Chinese, they can no more be viewed as chauvinists if they seek to promote Chinese language, culture and heritage.

When Prime Minister Goh Chok Tong and his colleagues took over in late 1990, they could not afford not to listen to the Chinese community; after all, Singapore has a democratic polity in which the Chinese account for over three-quarters of the electorate. The leaders of the Chinese-speaking, conscious of this critical fact, began to make special attempts to seek to improve the position, role and standing of their community from the late 1980s, when for all practical purposes Singapore had begun to be governed by the second-generation PAP rulers. In order to organise and mobilise the Chinese-speaking, they began openly to canvass issues which for long had been regarded taboo by all Singaporeans — the role and position of the Chinese, the Chineseness of Singapore and the place of Chinese language and culture.

A PAP member of parliament told this writer in December 1990 that the Chinese-speaking had

> . . . even begun to push the government because they believed that Goh Chok Tong, the new Prime Minister, was under special pressure to perform well at the next general elections, at the least maintain the level of popular vote secured by the PAP in the 1988 general elections.[4]

He added that the new second-generation PAP rulers, not being entirely confident about the level of support of the non-Chinese that they could attract (especially in view of its denial by many Malays in the 1988 general elections), could not afford to ignore the pressure from the Chinese-speaking. So long as Lee Kuan Yew had been Prime Minister, little special importance had been attached by the government to the Chinese vote and it had been allowed only minimal influence on the government's political and electoral calculations. Based upon its spectacular achievements in the economic sphere, the government then had full confidence that a vast majority of Chinese voters would continue backing the government. Furthermore, in those days, overawed by Prime Minister Lee Kuan Yew's special stature, extraordinary toughness and combativeness, few leaders of the Chinese-speaking had the courage to take on the government and attempt to "push" it on behalf of their community.

However, from the beginning, Prime Minister Goh Chok Tong and his colleagues had no choice but to attach far greater importance to the Chinese support for the government than did the first-generation PAP rulers. A top-ranking second-generation leader of the government told this writer in January 1989 (soon after the 1988 general elections which had resulted in a certain disenchantment with the Malays among PAP rulers as they suspected that many Malay voters had failed to support the government and instead had turned to opposition parties) that the government could no more afford to rely on Malay support:

> They cannot be depended upon. They are likely to remain disgruntled, not so much because of influences from outside Singapore, but because of their own inability to improve their position significantly. We can't make political calculations for the future depending upon continued strong political and electoral support from the Malays.[5]

He added that in view of this, the government would have to depend a great deal more on the support of the Chinese and especially seek to woo them. He also argued that in the past the Chinese community "had been allowed less than the Malays and the Indians with regard to the projection of their language, culture and heritage. This has to change. We are trying to achieve this now through our emphasis on a National Ideology".[6]

In the case of the indigenous Malays, the relationship between them and the PAP had come under more acute strain in the 1980s, especially in the late 1980s. According to a top-ranking Malay leader of the government, it had been precipitated by the following.[7] Firstly, the official visit to Singapore by the Israeli president had caused widespread anger among the Malays and a certain disenchantment with the government. The visit had generated an extreme reaction from the Malaysian Malays, especially across the causeway in Johore where at times effigies of PAP leaders were burnt and calls were made by some to stop the supply of water to Singapore. It is believed that if the Malaysian Malays had not reacted in such an extreme manner, possibly the Singaporean Malays would have tended to accept the visit, albeit grudgingly, without much excessive and publicly expressed anger. Clearly the reaction of the Malaysian Malays had placed the Singaporean Malays in a position in which, as good Muslims, they had little choice but to follow the lead given by their kith and kin.

Secondly, many Malays had begun to be seriously concerned about "the increasing reassertion of Chineseness in Singapore allowed by the government, often even sponsored by it" — the emphasis on the teaching of Mandarin, the Speak Mandarin Campaign, giving Chinese names to new townships and roads, etc. These were viewed as part of an overall pattern of deviation from the concept of multi-racialism devised and introduced in the 1960s. It was feared that the government's commitment to de-emphasise the Chineseness of Singapore had begun to erode and that this was inevitably to weaken the status and role of minorities in the future. The Malays were especially worried that the second-generation PAP leaders, devoid of the perspective and sensitivity of the first-generation leaders, were not as strongly committed to the continuing need to de-emphasise the Chineseness of Singapore and to persuade the Chinese to desist from behaving and acting as the dominant majority.

Thirdly, the Singaporean Malays, except for the older generation, had come to appreciate the fact that Singapore was a multi-racial entity in which they constituted only a minority and as such their *bumiputra* status could not mean the same as in neighbouring Malay-ruled Malaysia; they had begun to accept that in Singapore it could mean little more than a symbolic acknowledgement of them as the *bumiputra*. But to them that symbolic recognition was of special importance as it gave them a certain sense of self-importance and pride in an island that historically had been theirs. This had become a matter of major concern among the younger Malays who were fearful of losing their special status.

Fourthly, during the period, the exclusion of the Malays from the air force, the navy and certain sections of the army, which had been a part of government policy since decolonisation and independence, became a source of Malay anger and resentment when it was publicly discussed and argued by a prominent member of the government, Brigadier-General Lee Hsien Loong. So long as the policy had remained unpublicised and not widely known, the Malays had tended to understand it and not feel especially hurt. But once it had come to be publicly argued and defended, the Malays had to face publicly that the government did not seem to trust their loyalty to Singapore and that it was unwilling to jeopardise the security of the country by allowing them to join those services. The episode was seen as especially unfortunate by some Malay leaders of the PAP as it happened at a time when a small number of Malays had begun to be recruited to these sensitive parts of the defence forces from which they had been excluded in the past as a result of an initiative by Goh Chok Tong as Defence Minister.

Finally, suggestions by some leaders of the government, who had been especially influenced by eugenics, that in order to improve the general breed of Singaporeans and enhance ethnic coherence and harmony there had to be far greater acceptance of inter-ethnic marriages by all communities, were received with the greatest hostility by the Malays. The Malays were especially disappointed by the participation of Senior Minister Lee Kuan Yew in the debate. They were not only fearful of losing their distinctive identity as a people, but also of being pressured into compromising some key precepts of their Islamic religion.

On the whole, the Malays were entirely unable to understand some actions of the government. So was a leading pro-government journalist who chose to state with uncharacterstic forthrightness in a review of the year 1990, published by the influential and government-sponsored Institute of Policy Studies:

> Never since the dark days of communal politics when Singapore was a part of Malaysia had Singaporeans been made to feel so acutely aware of racial differences. This worried many Singaporeans. The blame was laid squarely at

the government's door. The perennial question posed was whether there was really a need, since the Herzog affair [the controversy surrounding the official visit by Israeli President Herzog], to keep making pronouncements and statements which kept race in the forefront of the public mind? Malays in the Singapore Armed Forces, bunching of Malays in primary schools, racial enclaves in housing estates, birth rate figures, Mr Lee's assertion that no Indian was likely to be accepted as Singapore's Prime Minister, etc. were all cited as examples.[8]

The Malay anger and disenchantment had been reflected in their reduced support for the PAP in the 1988 general elections. Two years later, when Goh Chok Tong took over as Prime Minister, he began attempts to improve the relationship with the Malays and engender among them a stronger sense of belonging to a multi-racial, *Singaporean* Singapore. In this he was able to take advantage of the strongly favourable image that he had among the Malays. He has been seen by the Malays as being able to understand their problems and take a constructive view and as willing to assist them. His extremely gentle personality and an entirely non-combative leadership style have contributed further to the confidence that many Malays have in the new Prime Minister. They have come to believe, despite their previous misgivings about the attitudes of second-generation PAP leaders towards them, that the new PAP government, due to his influence

> ... does not view the Malays, to the same extent as before, as the source of a lot of problems for Singapore and as being incapable of change and progress. The government has now begun to see the Malays as being capable of change and modernisation through education and skills.[9]

The process of reconciliation has also been facilitated by the fact that most Malays during the last few years have shown a new willingness to reconcile themselves to their changed circumstances and position in Singapore resulting from the separation of Singapore from the Malay-ruled Malaysia. The problem of their adjustment to an independent Singapore had been accentuated by the fact that they had been turned into a small, essentially powerless, minority in an island that was *theirs* historically and had been *Tanah Melayu* to them, even during the period of British rule when they themselves had wielded little real power and influence. It had come to be largely ruled by the Chinese whose domination over the island had long been resented by the Malays. The deep disappointment and anger at their changed fortunes had continued well into the 1970s. Their changing attitudes during the 1980s helped the government deal with the Malays and remove the sense of alienation among them.

When Prime Minister Goh Chok Tong and his colleagues assumed power in 1990, it was obvious, from the beginning, that they would take into account the significant changes in the social, economic, ethnic and geo-political environment, and seek to adapt and relate the founding principle of a multi-racial cultural democracy to the new Singapore realities. Their education and training as technocrats and their work experience, including that in the government, had especially prepared them for problem-solving: analysing and reviewing policies in order to adapt them to changing realities. Under their rule, the Singapore government has come to assume a greatly more interventionist role with regard to the management of ethnic diversity.

During the short period the second-generation leaders have been in power, the following seem to have emerged as the key purposes of their strategy for the management of ethnicity:

1. To continue to promote the Asianisation of Singapore, but with much enhanced vigour and giving special attention to the problem of deculturation among the Chinese.
2. To reduce disparities between ethnic groups by specially encouraging education and skills and by seeking to create for the Malays and the Indians a special place of their own in the modern economy of Singapore.

Before we look at these, it is important to note that under the new rulers of Singapore a significant change has taken place in the way the government deals with ethnicity and ethnic issues.

In the past, in view of Singaporeans' overly sharp ethnic sensitivities, their general lack of maturity in dealing with ethnic issues and the extreme threat posed by ethnic disharmony and conflict, especially the fear of it attracting intervention from the outside by the country's powerful neighbours, Malaysia and Indonesia, the government had no choice but to use considerable finesse in managing excessively emotion-laden ethnic issues and problems. During the early years, not being fully secure politically, the first-generation PAP rulers had developed the prudent approach of seeking to get around such problems rather than attempting to tackle them head-on. At times its leaders had even considered it preferable not to spell out their objectives explicitly to Singaporeans. S Rajaratnam, a pre-eminent first-generation leader, had told this writer some years back:

> We work on the basis that there is a wide gap between the collective and individual commitments of people. Individually they tend to be more pragmatic. In Singapore, many people still worry about their language and culture. But most of them still send their children to English-medium schools. When it comes to an individual's own child, he says: "If I send him to a Chinese school and he finishes it, what happens after that? Will he be able to become a doctor or a lawyer? Better send him to an English school."
>
> We satisfy their emotions by publicly having a policy which does not humiliate them, which is not totally contrary to their collective commitments. We tell them: "Yes, you can send your children to Chinese or Tamil schools and you can use Mandarin and Tamil wherever you like, including the parliament." When you are dealing with emotions, especially where they are right emotions, you never meet them head-on. You work your way around them. People don't keep on pushing a door that is open. We opened the door by adopting the policy that all languages and schools were equal and parents had the right to send children to the schools of their liking.[10]

The government, fearful of creating ethnic controversy and disharmony, had then tended to be extremely wary of "over-managing" ethnic issues; it had generally sought to keep visible and direct government intervention to the minimum. It believed that in managing ethnicity the paramount role of the state was

1. To ensure that contentious ethnic issues were not left unresolved to fester and precipitate public controversy and confrontation between the different communities.
2. To maintain a general environment of ethnic understanding, peace and amity that promoted mutual understanding and intermingling.

Beyond that, desired changes in ethnic attitudes and relationships had to be effected through minimal or disguised government intervention.

During the last few years, however, under Prime Minister Goh Chok Tong, the new PAP rulers have markedly changed their way of dealing with ethnic issues and problems. In certain ways, their largely technocratic background and the seemingly exaggerated confidence they have in their abilities as problem-solvers, have tended to give many of them a special disposition to be overly interventionist in regard to ethnic issues and problems. A prominent first-generation leader, S Rajaratnam, told this writer recently that even though they had indulged in a considerable amount of social engineering when they ruled Singapore, they had desisted from "attempting to manipulate ethnicity directly, as we knew it meant playing with fire. But the second-generation leaders show no such fears. They seem to believe that they can even manipulate the ethnic attitudes and behaviour of Singaporeans."[11]

Clearly, Prime Minister Goh Chok Tong and his colleagues have been influenced by their belief that Singaporeans have matured to the extent that a vast majority of them can handle ethnic issues without getting excessively angry and emotional and that today there is no real danger of ethnic confrontation and conflict. A top-ranking leader of the government told this writer recently:

> Today the situation has changed dramatically. The PAP has been solidly entrenched in power. There are no credible opposition parties that could make an effective challenge to its monopoly of power. The government's control

mechanisms have been in operation with such effectiveness that there is little chance of any serious ethnic disharmony and conflict. Therefore, the PAP government can take a more relaxed view and allow ethnicity to manifest itself more freely. The government can now take initiatives to deal directly with sensitive ethnic issues. It does not have to disguise its intent or actions in this regard. It can even allow community leaders to speak on behalf of their own different people and make demands.[12]

Prime Minister Goh Chok Tong himself told this writer in May 1991, soon after he had taken over as Prime Minister:

> In the last few years ... the government has intervened actively — in the case of the Chinese, to get the Chinese to speak Mandarin, to celebrate their cultural month, and for government leaders to be seen as patrons for certain Chinese organisations. Of course, when we do that for the Chinese, because of our commitment to multi-culturalism, we would do likewise for the Malays and the Indians.[13]

In the past, such direct and visible involvement in the affairs of the different communities by PAP members of parliament and government, especially those representing the Chinese majority, was frowned upon by the first-generation PAP rulers.

Asianising Singapore

The new PAP rulers of Singapore, who themselves have been the products of the special environment created by the policies of the government during the 1960s and the 1970s that were geared especially to creating an essentially English-speaking Singapore, believe that those policies had their greatest impact on the Chinese. If attempts were not urgently made to restore and enhance their distinctive identity and culture, the community might face the danger of losing its roots and vital heritage altogether and furthermore of being enervated. A senior first-generation leader told this writer recently that

> ... this exaggerated fear of many of the new leaders results from the fact that they look at the issue of deculturisation of the Chinese in personal terms. They are English-speaking and highly westernised and, during the last few years, they have come to develop a certain sense of guilt about it. When they are told by the leaders of the Chinese-speaking that the Chinese language, culture and identity are threatened, they readily accept their view. They tend to be on the defensive in any discussion of the issue with the Chinese-speaking. They are not able to stand up to them and argue as we did in the fifties and the sixties. We had faced the same problem, in an even more intense and explosive form. Abuses were hurled upon us and we were called enemies of Chinese culture and language. My fear is that our successors tend easily to panic in dealing with the Chinese-speaking.[14]

Prime Minister Goh Chok Tong and his colleagues consider the matter so vital that they have sought to go beyond their arguments of the 1980s that the Asianisation of Singapore was needed to save the values, cultures and heritages of Singaporeans, especially the Chinese, as well as to maintain a continuing high level of economic achievements by Singaporeans. The new imperatives presented by them relate essentially to the Chinese. Asked if the government's worry was that, of the three communities, the Chinese were losing a lot more than the others, Prime Minister Goh Chok Tong told this writer in May 1991: "Correct, correct. Indians possibly too. The Malays would not lose it. But the Chinese would."[15]

The new technocratic rulers, possessing a penchant for acute analysis and the special zealousness with which they tend to approach problem-solving, have found new, additional reasons for continuing the Asianisation of Singapore, including the restoration of the Chineseness of the Chinese. It is now argued that if the Chineseness of the Chinese in Singapore is not restored, Singapore would have to face several serious consequences. Firstly, Singapore is likely to lose many of its highly-educated and skilled citizens, who are the chief producers of wealth in the country. Secondly, as the Singapore polity is the most in harmony with the traditional political culture of the Chinese, it may have serious implications for political stability and the effective working of the polity in the future. Thirdly, it may cause the family system and the traditional sense of family responsibility to erode to such a degree that the government would come under pressure to assume new welfare responsibilities.

1. *Stopping the loss of highly-educated and skilled citizens*
Prime Minister Goh Chok Tong told this writer in May 1991 that many Chinese who are educated in English, in Singapore or overseas in western countries, think of emigrating when there is "the slightest hiccup over here". He maintained:

> Their bond with the country is not there because the bond with the community is not there. They become individual economic animals, looking for the greenest pasture in the world.
>
> Now, if that becomes a common phenomenon, where will Singapore be? The United States opens its doors to immigrants, Australia and New Zealand welcome more immigrants. I think quite a few of our Singaporeans would go, not just the cream, but also others with post-secondary education. It's this phenomenon that worries us. Our people must have certain emotional bonds with Singapore, and these bonds come from their own different cultures.
>
> And the other point is that if we define ourselves in terms of being Singaporeans, that relates only to a short civilisation. As independent Singaporeans, even shorter. So why give away the long link with the past? Why not be proud of our four to five thousand years of civilisation. That would give us pride — I am part of a new nation, but I am not a new man, I also have long traditions.[16]

For long in the past, it was believed by the PAP rulers that a multi-racial Singapore, with a widening common Singaporean identity and culture shared by all, would give their best educated and most productive citizens a strong enough sense of belonging to Singapore to make them remain in the country and contribute to its progress and prosperity. Most of these were highly westernised Chinese, the English-educated ersatz, who were not likely to be able to develop an emotional bond with Singapore based upon their Chinese culture and heritage. But now it is argued by the new rulers that the approach had not worked and that the only effective way an overriding sense of belonging to Singapore can be created among the Chinese members of this indispensable élite is by restoring the Chineseness of Singapore so that they are able to develop an emotional attachment to it. Prime Minister Goh Chok Tong told this writer in May 1991:

> It is a very important issue for us. We ask ourselves, ten, twenty years from now, what will Singapore be like? Is Singapore just a geographical entity populated by people of different outlooks, very superficial, or is it deeper, is it a nation?
> Like Taiwan, for example. The Taiwanese who went abroad to study in the United States, I understand that most of them go back to Taiwan because the culture in Taiwan is different from that in the United States. They go back, for if they stay in the United States they feel they have lost something.
> Now, if we don't create this sort of feeling for Singapore, Singaporeans who live abroad in Vancouver, California, Sydney or London will not notice the difference from being in Singapore — it's all the same. We don't want that to happen. If you stay outside, away from Singapore, you must feel that you miss something. Otherwise, we are going to lose more and more Singaporeans.[17]

The idea is that an emotional bond with Singapore should be created for the Chinese through Singapore's Chineseness, for the Indians through its Indianness and for the Malays through its Malayness. The new rulers are fully aware that as a general notion it sounds good, but in practice it creates a serious problem. As the Malays and the Indians constitute only small minorities, the Malayness of Singapore would relate essentially to the Malayness of certain areas of Malay concentration in Singapore and the Indianness would be reflected only in the Indianness of the so-called Little India. But the Chineseness of

Singapore cannot be limited only to certain pockets. The Chinese constitute over two-thirds of the population and, obviously, the Chineseness of Singapore would be the most visible, reflected in the entirety of Singapore. It is likely to effect the entire image of the nation as well as the state. That is why it needs to be handled with some care. Firstly, the increasing Chineseness of Singapore has to be carefully balanced by giving special attention to the promotion of Malayness and Indianness. Secondly, what is even more important is that the process is not allowed to lead to the manifestation of Chinese chauvinism. As Prime Minister Goh Chok Tong told this writer in May 1991: "Provided they [the Chinese] don't assert too much of the Chineseness and if they have a very tolerant attitude — then all will be well."[18]

There should be no question about the commitment of Prime Minister Goh Chok Tong and his colleagues to a genuinely multi-racial and multi-cultural Singapore. They possess, on the whole, as strong a sensitivity on issues of ethnicity as the first-generation founding fathers of Singapore. They are also equally fearful of the destructive potential of turning today's Singaporean Singapore into a Chinese Singapore. Even the Chinese-speaking business community, which in the past during the 1950s and the 1960s had provided some patrons of Chinese chauvinism, is influenced by the spectacular economic growth and prosperity of the last quarter century and shows full appreciation of the hazards of Chinese extremism; few of them today would wish to establish a Chinese Singapore. In the words of a prominent second-generation leader, the problem in this regard is essentially that

> . . . once you start restoring and strengthening the Chineseness of the Chinese in Singapore it is difficult to determine how far you can go. There is also the problem that once you have started the process and it has gained its own momentum and attracted widespread support from the Chinese, it may be very difficult to stop it at a given point.[19]

2. *Maintaining a stable political order*
It has also begun to be suggested by the new rulers that the restoration of the Chineseness of the Chinese may have a special

importance for the maintenance of a stable political order in Singapore. In this they seem to have been influenced by the thoughts of Senior Minister Lee Kuan Yew. It is maintained that Chinese culture and heritage, based on Confucianism, represent a distinctive view of government and rulers which is of special relevance to Singapore. So long as a government proves to perform well and promote the well-being of its people, the Chinese tend to accept its legitimacy fully and allow it to govern freely. They tend to take the practical view that any disruptive political action by the people will only make it much more difficult for the government to perform with the greatest effectiveness and promote the well-being of the people. For them, the authority of the rulers to rule and its acceptance by them have to be based upon the former's performance and achievements. A government, as stated by Senior Minister Lee Kuan Yew, that does not perform effectively and deliver the good life inevitably loses its legitimacy and gets challenged by the people and toppled.[20] In all, the Chinese, according to Senior Minister Lee Kuan Yew, have a "consensus-seeking culture".

A stable political order is considered vital for the survival of Singapore. Its past economic achievements were based on that and its future progress and prosperity have to depend on that. It is believed by the new rulers that the political culture of the Malays and the Indians is distinctively different from that of the Chinese. The political attitudes and behaviour of the Malays, based in their Islamic religion, and that of the Indians, influenced excessively by their experience of an especially long and damaging period of alien rule, tend to be more given to producing political confrontation, disruption and drama. The Malays and the Indians tend to be more easily excitable. Therefore, they cannot be entirely relied upon to show the same sense of pragmatism towards the government as the Chinese and be fully involved in the "consensus-seeking" political style of the Chinese.

In 1992, at the end of an official visit to Pakistan, Senior Minister Lee Kuan Yew emphasised the role played by the "consensus-seeking culture" of Singapore in the achievement of immense economic progress and prosperity. He had contrasted it with that of Pakistan that created "constant sniping, barrage after barrage. After the sniping is over, then endless feuding".[21] He had maintained that it was Singapore's good fortune that it had a predominantly consensus-seeking culture. He gave the example of the different stances and styles of Chinese and non-Chinese opposition leaders. Though Singapore Democratic Party leader Chiam See Tong and the Workers' Party representative in parliament might have disagreed with the government over certain issues, the differences were within reasonable limits, and were over how to solve problems, not whether the problems existed. In contrast, the Workers' Party leader, J B Jeyaretnam, had a totally different viewpoint from the government on all issues. Senior Minister Lee had added: "Now supposing instead of being Lee, I'm a Singham or something, all our time we'll be putting in mortar shells and lobbing each other. No work will be done and the ground will be totally confused."[22] Asked if the non-consensus-seeking culture and attitudes in Pakistan could be changed, he said that he too had reflected on the problem as South Asians constituted about seven per cent of Singapore's population. But he added that the South Asians in Singapore had been acclimatised into the consensus-seeking framework of the larger population, the Chinese, and jokingly pointed out that they still wrote more letters to the newspapers than others.

It is believed that both the Malays and the Indians can be far more concerned with norms, in the case of the Malays derived from their Islamic religion and in the case of the Indians based upon the borrowed western precepts of democracy, justice and equality. Even if the government is performing well and promoting the well-being of the people, they can still be dissatisfied and be critical of it in terms of the values they hold dear. These aspects of their political culture are not viewed as being especially conducive to the creation of a stable political order and a political system that works and makes impressive achievements.[23] Many years back, in 1982, when these matters were not easily discussed in Singapore, S Rajaratnam told this writer:

> The Chinese are more pragmatic in the sense that they are less interested in abstract ideas in politics. They are primarily interested in knowing if your policy would

damage their interests. For example, about one man one vote. They would ask you: what does it mean in terms of policy? We say, one man one vote means that the rich should be taxed to pay for the poor. Then he would readily say: "I don't think it is a very good idea." But if one man one vote does not mean that, he will be all for one man one vote. But the Indian will start the other way round. He will say: "I believe in one man one vote, doesn't matter what."[24]

It is argued by the new rulers that restoring the Chineseness of the Chinese is essential to ensuring continued political stability in Singapore. The Chinese, who remain wedded to their traditional values and the political attitudes towards government derived from them, have to be given a central place in the Singapore polity. They have to continue to constitute the core of the Singapore population so that their political behaviour and attitudes continue to provide the vital underpinnings for a stable political order and that they mitigate against political turbulence, disruption and drama.[25] For this reason, the government has sought to ensure, despite concern and criticism expressed by the non-Chinese, that its immigration and other related policies remain geared to maintaining the present ethnic distribution of Singapore's population.

3. *Restoring the traditional family system*
A top-ranking second-generation leader of the PAP told this writer recently: "Family should be at the core of the Singapore society".[26] The government today considers it vital to ensure that a rejuvenated family system, based on a strong traditional sense of family responsibilities, should continue to take care of the varied welfare functions, otherwise they would inevitably have to be undertaken by the government, thereby diminishing its ability that much to concentrate on the promotion of economic expansion and growth. The government does not want to involve itself at all with welfare functions, such as looking after the elderly and the others who cannot take care of themselves. These must remain the primary responsibility of families. They maintain that the western influences in the past have tended to produce excessive individualism at the cost of the traditional

concern for and commitment to the family and the community. In this regard, the government considers it necessary to give special attention to the Chinese as they are the ones who have absorbed the greatest amount of western influence.

The PAP rulers have an acute dread of the welfare state based upon the experience in the West. They always point to the damage wrought by welfarestatism in New Zealand, a relatively large country with a small population and immense natural resources, that during the past quarter century has slid from being one of the richest, offering its people a high quality of life, to being overtaken by some of the newly industrialised Asian countries.

Even though Prime Minister Goh Chok Tong and his colleagues have tried hard to be even-handed in their attempt to Asianise Singapore and have provided as much assistance to the Malays and the Indians as to the Chinese to be able to maintain and enhance their own distinctive identities and cultures, their programme has created some suspicion and disquiet among the non-Chinese during the past few years. Some Malays and Indians have feared that the government's agenda could lead to an erosion of some of the core components of the strategy for the management of ethnicity that had been devised by the first-generation rulers during the 1960s. Some of them have even suggested that the new PAP rulers have been more willing to listen to the Chinese majority and that they are not being fully mindful of the possible effects of their programme of Asianising Singapore, especially its component of restoring the Chineseness of the Chinese, on the founding principle of a multi-racial cultural democracy that enshrined the principle of equality of status and rights for all the different ethnic components.

The suspicions and concerns of the Malays and the Indians were especially intense during the period from 1989 to 1993. During this period, almost all Malays and Indians that this writer talked with in Singapore raised the issue of the future of their respective communities. Reviewing the year 1990, a prominent Singapore journalist wrote in a publication of the influential Institute of Policy Studies:

What complicated matters further was the government's frequent reiteration of the need to combat certain harmful western cultural influences, such as excessive individualism ... Its emphasis on Singapore remaining an Asian society and its references to Confucian values were seen by some as insidious attempts at Sinicising Singapore. The suspicion lurked in the minds of many from the minority communities and coloured their perception of otherwise innocuous statements or policies.

But the unhappiness was by no means confined only to the non-Chinese. Many largely English-educated Chinese Singaporeans were also fearful that all the talk about imbibing more Asian values, which they saw as a codeword for Chinese/Confucian values, meant their children would be made to spend more time studying Chinese. And the more politicised among them again saw the continued emphasis on Confucian values as possibly another attempt to make Singaporeans more respectful and obedient towards authority.[27]

The fears of the Malays and the Indians were further aggravated by the following.

Following the general election in late 1991, in which the overall popular support of the government had slightly declined, there was considerable, highly excited public discussion and debate, led by senior leaders of the government, about the feelings and grievances of the Chinese-speaking. The controversy began on 16 September when the Chinese-speaking Deputy Prime Minister, Ong Teng Cheong, in an extremely forthright speech to the Chinese Press Club, gave full expression to the emotions and frustrations of the Chinese-speaking. He suggested that the Chinese-speaking felt that the government had ignored their concerns and problems and that they had signalled their unhappiness through the ballot box. He asserted:

> The Chinese-educated . . . feel that their concern and worries over the Chinese language and culture have not attracted the due attention of the government. They feel that although the government kept mentioning the

importance of learning the mother tongue, it has not given serious attention and care to the use of the Chinese language and development of the Chinese culture.[28]

He added:

The Chinese-educated have often wondered if they are there only to be pushed around. Why can't they have the right to take part in policy decision-making? But they keep their grievances to themselves, and have become the neglected 'silent majority'.[29]

The following day, in an interview with *The Straits Times*, Deputy Prime Minister Ong Teng Cheong further elaborated his concern: "If the government only wishes to fulfil the needs and aspirations of the English-educated and only develop one aspect of the society and is biased against the others, then it may lose the support of the others".[30] He maintained that traditionally a majority of the Chinese-speaking had supported the PAP and had accepted the rise of English as the working language of Singapore. But now they felt that the government had come to take their support for granted and that it had been paying more attention to the vocal English-educated: "They feel that, with English taking such a dominant role in society and the English-educated holding all the important jobs, opportunities to rise are closed off to them."[31] He argued that the decline in the popular vote of the PAP was a result of the widespread unhappiness among the Chinese-speaking.

Within a few days, Senior Minister Lee Kuan Yew chose to make an even stronger statement. His intervention, based upon his special status as the founding father of modern Singapore, was able to transform Ong Teng Cheong's complaint, made essentially on behalf of the Chinese-speaking, into an urgent national imperative.[32] Speaking to Singapore journalists in Alma Ata in Kazakhstan on 22 September, he said that the views of those in the Singapore cabinet who were close to the rank and file of the Chinese community and who spoke their language would carry more weight as they represented the larger segment of the population, and that the government would have to give special attention to the Chinese-speaking who formed the "silent majority".[33]

Echoing the sentiments of Ong Teng Cheong, Senior Minister Lee Kuan Yew maintained that the Chinese-speaking were beginning to feel that even though they constituted a majority, they were being ignored and neglected because the government was more interested in the English-educated and the Malays. "They felt that this was getting out of focus. They were saying: 'What about our worries and about how we are losing our sense of place, language and sense of identity and culture?' It is a reminder that they cannot be taken for granted."[34] He added: "I think it was a sense of being squeezed out of the mainstream, that they were no longer getting the kind of attention that as the majority community they should have. I think that caused the switch."[35]

Senior Minister Lee Kuan Yew agreed that the government had paid undue attention to the English-educated in the past because they were the ones who were most articulate and vocal in making demands and expressing their unhappiness. He noted that in the cabinet only he himself, Deputy Prime Ministers Ong Teng Cheong and Lee Hsien Loong, and Foreign Minister Wong Kan Seng spoke Mandarin and read the Chinese daily, *Lianhe Zaobao*, every day. He maintained that the undue attention on the English-educated had resulted from the reading habits of the ministers. "We came to the conclusion that the English-speaking were becoming the majority but in fact they were not. And the silent majority decided to remind us that this was not so."[36] The Chinese-speaking will continue to be the majority for the next ten to fifteen years at least.

Following this, considerable public debate and discussion ensued in Singapore. There was a general flurry of demands made on behalf of the Chinese-speaking. Some of these Chinese-speaking leaders, who in the past had failed to secure political prominence and positions because of their background, indulged in a bit of posturing as they viewed the controversy as an opportunity for them to boost their own political fortunes. Newspapers, especially the Chinese-language ones, were full of stories and comments about the special problems faced by the Chinese community, relating to Chinese language and culture and the plight of the Chinese-speaking.

The government, led by Prime Minister Goh Chok Tong, did not see it as a problem that was specifically based upon language and ethnicity, and it refused to panic. Prime Minister Goh Chok Tong, responding to the controversy, said on 22 September 1991 that it was important to understand that those who voted against the PAP did so not because they were Chinese-educated, but because they belonged to the low-income group. He acknowledged that to the Chinese-speaking he might have seemed to be moving too fast and to be trying to reach out to the English-speaking yuppies and professionals.[20] Some of his government's policies, according to him, might not have appealed to "the lower-income group whose main concerns are essentially bread and butter issues."[38] But, he stressed, this did not mean that the government had neglected "the Chinese ground." He said that he had emphasised before the election that the government was going to focus its policies "on the lower 80 per cent of Singaporeans".[39] As these policies had yet to be implemented, obviously the Chinese-speaking had felt neglected. Explaining that it was not possible to meet the aspirations of all Singaporeans at the same time, he had chosen to reach out to different groups "sequentially". In the past, he had sought to help the Malays, even though he knew that the Chinese would feel neglected. He said: "I know in my heart that it was a matter of time before I reached out to them [the Chinese-speaking], but they did not know."[40] Clearly, Prime Minister Goh Chok Tong was unwilling to accept that the dissatisfaction with the government among the Chinese-speaking had anything to do with their language and ethnic background and that it was based on their view that the government had not done enough for the Chinese and their language and culture.

A senior member of the government told this writer recently that Senior Minister Lee Kuan Yew had obviously over-reacted in acknowledging and highlighting the so-called problems faced by the Chinese-speaking.[41] He maintained that it was important to note that the government, headed by Prime Minister Goh Chok Tong, chose not to over-react. Its only response was to do "a few little things to pacify and quieten some of the leaders of the Chinese-educated" immediately after the issue had become a matter of public controversy. According to him, the problem had little to do with Chinese identity, language and culture. It was essentially class-based, but it had been presented as an ethnic issue by some leaders of the Chinese-speaking.

Another leader of the PAP, who is himself Chinese-speaking, told this writer recently:

> The issue of the Chinese-speaking which had been projected very forcefully by Deputy Prime Minister Ong Teng Cheong and Senior Minister Lee Kuan Yew immediately after the 1991 general elections was not really that serious a matter. It was unfortunate that it had been raised so forcefully at the time and had been allowed to become a matter of public controversy. Clearly, the problem had been canvassed in exaggerated terms by some leaders of the Chinese-speaking, who possibly had their own special reasons. It is interesting that none of them now is raising the issue. They are all quiet now. They are all doing very well and they do not seem interested in the "problem" any more. Even with regard to the language, culture and identity of the Chinese, it is all very quiet. Nobody is showing any more concerns about them and making any special demands.[42]

He added that the real concerns of the ordinary Chinese-speaking relate essentially to the issue of cost of living and cost of government services; these have begun to manifest themselves strongly once again. "At the moment, they do not have their Chinese-speaking leaders pushing them into excessively worrying about their language, culture and heritage and their lack of power and influence in the government."[43]

Despite the fact that Prime Minister Goh Chok Tong and his government had refused to show any excessive concern with regard to the complaints and grievances of the Chinese-speaking and make a panic response, the whole episode did create concern among the Malays and the Indians. During the following year or so in Singapore, most Malays and Indians showed an extreme sense of fear that the political pressure generated on behalf of the Chinese-speaking could easily result in attempts to turn

Singapore into an essentially Chinese Singapore. As they had the greatest respect for and total confidence in Senior Minister Lee Kuan Yew, they were bewildered by the unqualified support he had given to Deputy Prime Minister Ong Teng Cheong's complaint on behalf of the Chinese-speaking.

Moved by the fears and concerns of the Malays and the Indians, S Rajaratnam, one of the closest first-generation associates of Senior Minister Lee Kuan Yew, chose to give an unprecedented, extreme warning through an open letter, published in *The Straits Times* on 27 September:

> I believe that, contrary to my long-held conviction that all is well with the world, Pandora's box has now been opened.
>
> There is less reason now for me to believe that what is now happening in India, Sri Lanka, Yugoslavia and even the Soviet Union, cannot happen in Singapore.
>
> I am not so sure now that the immunity an independent Singapore enjoyed against contending communalism for 26 years is secure.
>
> When a "silent majority", embracing 77.7 per cent of the population, believes that its ethnic future is in jeopardy, how much more trembling there must be among Malays, Indians and Eurasians that their Singapore identity is any more secure; that the Singapore flag which symbolised that identity is nothing more than a fluttering in the wind.[44]

These angry words, reflecting deep hurt and concern, were written by one of the founding fathers of modern Singapore. It should not be difficult to imagine the depth of the impact of the episode on the rank and file of the minority communities.

It is important, however, to recognise that the concerns of the Chinese-speaking have not been entirely without foundation. Before we look at their grievances and their wishes, it would be useful to have an understanding of the nature of the community of the Chinese-speaking. It essentially is composed of three groups:

1. A small group of highly-educated, bilingual Chinese who speak and understand English and as a result have been able

to function with considerable ease in the English-speaking environment of Singapore and secure, without much difficulty, high-paid jobs.
2. Chinese, with secondary education at the old Chinese-medium schools (some of them having furthered their education at the now defunct Nanyang University), whose extremely limited knowledge of English has made it difficult for them to realise their full potential in respect of employment and status.
3. The dialect-speaking Chinese who have little understanding of English.

The problems faced by the first two groups, constituting a significant and influential part of the Chinese-speaking, are not extreme. As they are bilingual and they possess useful skills, they have generally done quite well, though not as well as the English-speaking. However, they are the ones who provide the leadership of the Chinese-speaking at the various levels and who articulate their grievances and anger. Their own frustrations are based on the belief, firstly, that they are discriminated against in employment, especially in regard to advancement in their careers, and secondly, that they have been kept out of the Singapore ruling class that has been monopolised by the English-speaking.

Serious problems are chiefly faced by the dialect-speaking third group. They have little knowledge of English and they are able to converse with their non-Chinese compatriots only through the rudimentary *Pasar* Malay that they have picked up. They have no specially useful skills and that makes it difficult for them to fit into the modern economy of Singapore and earn a reasonable living. In a way, their plight relates not to their being Chinese-speaking, but to being a part of the Singapore underclass. A prominent leader of the Chinese-speaking maintains that these deeply alienated Chinese account for some sixteen per cent of their community.[45] They believe that their problems, emanating from their position as the underclass, have attracted little attention of the government. He suggests that they have been especially angered by the fact that the government has been attempting to assist the poor and the under-achievers among the non-Chinese, especially the Malays, but not them. The élitist system of Singapore does not allow them a fair deal. Their shift from the old rural areas to the Housing Development Board estates has made things difficult for them. In the rural areas, they did not have to pay many government charges and they were often able to grow their own food. In the HDB flats they cannot grow their own food and they have to pay a wide variety of government charges, including excessive parking fees.

According to a prominent leader of the Chinese-speaking, the discontent among the Chinese-speaking has been accentuated by the commitment of the English-speaking rulers of Singapore to an extreme user-pay market economy. The economic system created by the English-speaking hurts them deeply — COE on cars and motor cycles, levy on foreign workers, increase in education fees, cost of health services. They believe that the system represents more western individualism than the communitarianism of the Chinese-speaking.[46] The Chinese-speaking are said to have a more caring attitude and tend to be concerned about the adverse impact on the poor of the market-based cost recovery policies of the government. In this regard, they are especially concerned about the government's continuing programme of privatisation of schools and hospitals, which has made their services to them more expensive. They are fearful that eventually, in the name of competition and efficiency, the government's privatisation programme will be extended to include housing and transport, inevitably making access to them more expensive.

The Chinese-speaking, on the whole, do not feel too happy with the English-speaking Chinese for the latter urge them to learn and speak Mandarin, but they themselves do not practice what they preach. According to a prominent leader of the Chinese-speaking, the contradictions between the Chinese-speaking and the English-speaking are far more serious than those between the Chinese and the non-Chinese.[47] The English-speaking since independence have constituted the ruling class and "they have always been hostile to the Chinese-speaking, considering us to being conservative, non-modern, left wing, superstition-ridden and clannish."[48] Based upon the memories of how their people had been treated by PAP governments during the early years of their rule, the Chinese-speaking still live under the fear that they can again be branded as Chinese chauvinists and become the target for harsh treatment by the English-speaking rulers.

On the whole, the recent attempts by the government to give special attention to the Chinese-speaking and their aspirations and grievances has considerably improved its relationship with them. However, the Chinese-speaking still retain their traditional suspicions about the English-speaking and do not regard them as a part of their "community". A group of editors and senior journalists of Chinese language newspapers in Singapore, who are especially close to the community, recently outlined the following to this writer as representing the feelings and aspirations of the Chinese-speaking, as to "what they want":[49]

1. They want the government to give the Chinese-speaking greater recognition and attention, including representation in the government (the parliament and the ministry) as well as administration at all levels. To make it possible for the Chinese-speaking to be able to deal with government departments without any fear and hesitation, they would like more Chinese-speaking officials at public counters. They also want the government to appoint more Chinese-speaking to government committees and commissions so that their distinctive views, values and aspirations are more fully reflected in the advice received by the government.
2. Until the formation of the Chinese Development Assistance Council recently, they were dissatisfied that the government had not seen it fit to establish a MENDAKI-like organisation for the Chinese. They believe that there are large numbers of Chinese who face problems similar to those faced by the Malays and who need similar assistance. They maintain that among their families the education of their children is adversely affected by their economic situation. As in their case, both the husband and wife (often even the older children) have to work, their children's education tends to get neglected, resulting in poor performance by many of them.
3. They feel quite unhappy that when they express their

concerns with regard to their Chinese heritage, language and culture and make demands in respect of them, they tend to be branded as Chinese chauvinists, but when the Malays do the same it is regarded as entirely legitimate and proper. In this regard, they consider it significant that they are criticised and condemned less by their Malay and Indian compatriots than by the English-speaking Chinese. It is their belief that the Malays and the Indians generally tend to be more understanding and sympathetic to their aspirations with regard to their language, culture and heritage.

4. They maintain that after decolonisation the Chinese had acted exemplarily in agreeing to a multi-racial, multi-cultural and multi-lingual Singapore that de-emphasised the Chineseness of Singapore and accorded equal rights and status to the ethnic minorities and a special position to the indigenous Malays. They feel disappointed that the minorities, instead of being thankful to the Chinese and applauding their fairmindedness, are quick to criticise them if they make any demands on behalf of their own community.

5. Generally they hold strong feelings against the English-speaking Chinese, who, they believe, criticise them for making demands on behalf of the Chinese community, its culture and language, in order to maintain and strengthen their own social, cultural, linguistic and political dominance. But the English-speaking Chinese are shrewd enough to present their criticism as being on behalf of the Malay and Indian minorities and for the protection of modern Singapore's multi-racial and multi-cultural foundations. In doing that they misrepresent the Chinese-speaking as being unfair to the minorities and wanting to create a Chinese Singapore.

6. The issues of Chinese language and culture do not constitute a matter of extreme concern among the Chinese-speaking any more. In the 1960s, these issues caused a great deal of anger, controversy and turmoil because they were then championed by the communists and the pro-communists. The PAP government then, in order to stop the communists from exploiting them for their own political purposes, had prohibited any public discussion of these issues. The result was that widespread anger and frustration had festered for

long among the Chinese-speaking for not being able to express their feelings openly and lend their support to their community's language and culture, which to them constituted the very essence of their being. Now that these issues are allowed to be discussed more freely, they have lost their special attraction. In view of the commitment of the government since the early 1980s to especially promoting and enhancing the cultures and heritages of all the different peoples, the Chinese-speaking have come to have a greatly relaxed view on the issues. However, deep concern remains alive among them with regard to the increasing westernisation of the young Chinese. They believe that even though they all speak Mandarin, as it is a compulsory subject, they are not absorbing the vital Chinese values and heritage and are fast losing their Chineseness. Mandarin is not working as an instrument to inculcate among them traditional Chinese values, thought, behaviour and way of life.

7. They are strongly opposed to the unduly excessive emphasis that the government has placed on English since independence. They appreciate the efforts of the government, since the early 1980s, to promote Mandarin among the Chinese, but they believe that this should have been done from the beginning, before damage had been done to the Chinese community and its language through the state-sponsored excessive use of English. They maintain that the emphasis on English has gone too far and it is time that the government radically changes its view.

The vast new opportunities for Singapore to gain profitable commercial and other economic ties with China that came in the wake of the radical changes in the latter's economic direction and policies had clearly brought the two countries extremely close. Relations between the two countries had been good during the 1980s, but they had been restricted almost entirely to official contacts. There had been visits to each other's country by members of government, ministers and members of parliament. But there was extremely restricted and controlled movement of people, businessmen and academics.

At the beginning of the 1990s, it looked, certainly to the non-

Chinese, as if the floodgates had been opened. There ensued an unprecedented sudden movement of people between the two countries, including businessmen, technocrats, government servants, academics, students and political leaders. The new economic relationship opened up immense new opportunities for the Chinese-speaking, especially for the better-educated and businessmen among them. For years, being Chinese-speaking, they had come to feel marginalised in the expanding modern economy of Singapore. They had felt that their limited knowledge of English and their essentially traditional Chinese ways had made it extremely difficult for them to take as much advantage of the opportunities offered by the fast-growing economy of Singapore as the English-speaking who had fully cultivated the western ways. Thus they had serious worries about their future in the increasingly internationalised economy of Singapore, of being sidelined and becoming economically irrelevant. In their case, to start with, there was undoubtedly an element of sentiment and euphoria involved in the economic and commercial relationship with China.

The fast-growing relationship and contact with China soon began to transform the Chineseness of Singapore (which for the sake of the country's acceptance and survival in the Malay world of Southeast Asia had been disguised and de-emphasised for a quarter century) from an unavoidable and unfortunate liability to an important and immensely profitable asset. It began to give a new fillip to the learning and use of Mandarin. It brought to the surface, especially among the Chinese-speaking, a strong sense of pride in their Chineseness. Being totally Chinese came to be entirely "beautiful". An Economics lecturer at the National University of Singapore publicly proclaimed that he would speak nothing but Mandarin when he dealt with departments and agencies of the Singapore government.

Some Chinese, including a few of the lesser leaders of the PAP, began to talk of a Greater China, essentially in economic and commercial terms.[50] The idea had originally been initiated in Taiwan. Some in the Chinese community even began to talk, though not publicly, the logic of the strength of their numbers in Singapore: the Chinese accounted for more than three-quarters of the population and there was no reason why the fact should not be reflected in their status as well as in the Chineseness of Singapore.

This burgeoning new relationship and contact with China, and the seeming preoccupation with it in Singapore, of the government as well as the mass media, proved to be considerably unnerving to the Malay and Indian minorities. They began to worry about the continuing commitment of the Chinese majority to the founding principle of a multi-racial cultural democracy established in the 1960s and their own position and future in Singapore. They got themselves into such an extreme mood of uncertainty that even the visits to China by Senior Minister Lee Kuan Yew during this period and the speeches made by him in a variety of countries, seeking to explain the policies and compulsions of the government in Beijing and pleading with the West to show greater understanding, tended to compound their fears of their Singaporean Singapore being turned into a Chinese Singapore.

The Malays and the Indians had always viewed Senior Minister Lee Kuan Yew, who had battled relentlessly against Chinese chauvinists and communists during the 1950s and the 1960s, as the embodiment of a multi-racial Singapore and the most powerful protector of their rights and status. When the generational change of PAP rulers took place in 1990, they were relieved that Lee Kuan Yew continued to be associated with the governing of Singapore as a Senior Minister. They had been fearful that, not possessing the exceptional *mana* and political skills of the first-generation rulers, the new, younger and strongly technocratic second-generation leadership might not show the same courage and fortitude in standing up against Chinese chauvinists and extremists and that some of them might even be tempted to seek to appease the Chinese to secure their electoral backing. As such they had apprehensions about depending entirely on the second-generation rulers for their own place in the sun. Even though their fears were mostly based on their own perception rather than the reality of the attitudes and commitments of the second-generation leaders, they did add to their concerns and fears. In the circumstance, they were deeply perplexed by some of the recent analyses and advice by Senior Minister Lee Kuan Yew with regard to the problems of the

Chinese-speaking and the single-mindedness with which he had tended to support their cause. During the same period of heightened ethnic sensitivity, many of the Malays and the Indians were deeply saddened by the remarks made by Senior Minister Lee Kuan Yew, who, using his special privilege to be entirely candid and forthright on ethnic issues, had sought to indulge in negative stereotyping of them.

Soon Prime Minister Goh Chok Tong and his colleagues came to show some concern about the impact of the fast expanding commercial relationship and contact with China on domestic ethnic relationships as well as Singapore's relationship with its partners in ASEAN, especially Malaysia and Indonesia. Through a number of speeches, Prime Minister Goh Chok Tong sought to assure the non-Chinese about their future and attempted to soothe their feelings of hurt and concern. To deal with the situation further, the government sought to expand and strengthen Singapore's economic and commercial links with other ASEAN countries by promoting greater Singapore investments in them. It began to explore the possibilities of developing a trade relationship with Vietnam. It placed a special emphasis on building a special economic relationship with India, including the possibility of large Singapore investments. The government established a special office to encourage and facilitate the recruitment of highly qualified Indian expatriates to work in Singapore. In January 1994, Prime Minister Goh Chok Tong visited India to be the chief guest at the Republic Day Celebrations; this was the first time that an ASEAN head of government had been invited to be the chief guest on India's Republic Day. On his return, he began to talk of encouraging an "India fever" in Singapore similar to the "China fever" of the past few years.

Fortunately, for the government the controversy did not last long. Much of the anxiety among the non-Chinese during the episode had emanated more from the extreme concerns expressed by two senior ministers in the government and the resultant noisy demands made by a small group of leaders of the Chinese-speaking than any actions and policies of the government. The prolonged public preoccupation with the controversy had been kept alive, it is alleged, largely by the

Chinese language newspapers which had seen in it an opportunity to raise issues which had formed a part of their special crusade for at least the past 40 years. The result was that as soon as some of the leaders of the Chinese-speaking were able to gain special attention from the government as well as take advantage of the new opportunities offered to them by the fast-expanding commercial relationship with China, the controversy suddenly disappeared from the national agenda. A Chinese-speaking leader of the PAP told this writer recently:

> Highly educated Chinese-speaking, who are also bilingual, have found immense new opportunities for themselves as senior executives in businesses resulting from the vastly expanding trade relationship with China. Even Chinese-speaking middle-managers are in great demand with Singapore businesses to work for them in China. Many of them have even started their own businesses in China. Most of these are former graduates of Nanyang University. As a result, much of the long-standing deep dissatisfaction and resentment among them has all but disappeared. They are now preoccupied with running businesses or working for them and they now show little interest in the grievances of the Chinese-speaking.[51]

Ameliorating Inter-Ethnic Disparities

The strategy for the management of ethnicity devised in the 1960s accorded the different ethnic segments the right to maintain their distinctive identities, languages, religions and cultures and guaranteed them equal status and rights. It also included as a key element the maintenance of continuing economic expansion and growth. These were then seen as providing the necessary bases for a multi-racial Singaporean Singapore and ethnic peace, harmony and amity. At the time, most Singaporeans were relatively poor and therefore the question of disparities between ethnic groups did not constitute a serious issue; it did not attract any special attention of the government with regard to its strategy for the management of ethnicity.

Today, Prime Minister Goh Chok Tong and his colleagues believe that the strategy for the management of ethnicity has to go beyond that of the past. Continuing economic growth in itself may not be enough. They are fearful that disparities between ethnic segments may eventually provoke disharmony and create serious political problems in the future. They cannot afford to allow economic disparities to constitute the bases for serious ethnic grievances and discontent. Thus Prime Minister Goh Chok Tong's new government has chosen to go beyond the strategy of the 1960s and it now attaches special importance to at least removing the impediments that in the past had made it difficult for many Singaporeans to achieve their full potential in respect of education and skills and employment and had inevitably relegated them to the status of an underclass.

This special emphasis of Prime Minister Goh Chok Tong and his colleagues does not represent either a new idea or a new direction with regard to management of ethnic diversity in Singapore. The PAP rulers had been concerned about disparities in the past, but, as we noted in the last chapter, their concern then, firstly, had only been minimal, and secondly, had related essentially to the position of the indigenous Malay community.

Even though a small group of Singaporeans, consisting mostly of the English-speaking, earned very high incomes, the government had then shown little concern about the disparities, not only in terms of incomes but also in relation to power and position, between the English-speaking and the Chinese-speaking. This situation was deeply resented by the Chinese-speaking, but at the time they had tended to avoid any extreme public expression of their unhappiness. Moreover, since most Chinese-speaking had consistently given their support to the PAP, the government had little reason to worry about them. Similarly, since most Indians had continued to support the PAP loyally, they also had failed to attract any special attention from the government with regard to the growing disparities between them and the Chinese. Furthermore, Indians had been fairly well represented in the class of the high-income Singaporeans through those in the professions and the civil service, and this had tended to give the rank and file of their community a certain illusory sense of their powerfulness.

In respect of the Malays, however, the government could not then afford to ignore altogether the problem of disparities. Their indigenousness and the attitudes of Singapore's neighbours, Malaysia and Indonesia, had then made it imperative for the government to ensure that the Singaporean Malays were not unduly unhappy and dissatisfied with PAP rule. But even in their case, the government's concern about disparities between them and the Chinese was not as strong as it is today under Prime Minister Goh Chok Tong. The fear then had essentially been in terms of the future, that the Malays might not be able to take enough advantage of available opportunities and that the gap between them and the Chinese might continue to widen and eventually become a source of serious ethnic disharmony. A pre-eminent leader of the present government told this writer in mid-1983:

> For the next 20 years or so we may not have too much of a problem as the Malays, starting from their present base, are bound to improve their position significantly. They are already advancing from two-room to three-room Housing Development Board flats. It is certain that for the next two decades or so they will make tangible and visible improvements in their position and their standards of living. But after that they are going to find it exceedingly difficult to make further significant advances as it will become much more competitive. We fear that their progress will slow down and an increasingly glaring disparity between them and the Chinese will emerge that could easily develop into a source of serious discontent among them.[52]

The government's lack of a much stronger commitment to the Malays then had also been influenced by the fact that not many among the PAP rulers had any real confidence in the ability and commitment of the Malays to be able to achieve major improvements in their position. There was in this a certain element of prejudice based on the Malay stereotype created by the British colonial rulers. Their view had also been based mostly on the record of achievements of the Malays since independence. A pre-eminent second-generation leader of the government had told this writer some years back:

> Undoubtedly, Singapore Malays have changed to a degree. They are able to acquire certain skills, become technicians. In the universities, however, the Malays, who have been doing well and then going on professions or higher levels of the public service, have tended to be only part-Malay. Many of them are part-Indian or part-Arab.[53]

Today, Prime Minister Goh Chok Tong and his colleagues are far more deeply concerned not only about the disparities between the indigenous Malays and the Chinese, but also about those between the Indians and the Chinese as well as those, within the Chinese community, between the Chinese-speaking and the English-speaking. The spectacular economic achievements and prosperity of the past quarter century have made the disparities more glaring and have tended to make Prime Minister Goh Chok Tong and his colleagues more sensitive to the position and plight of the ordinary, not rich Singaporeans, irrespective of their ethnic background. Their own new outlook, distinctively different from that of the first-generation rulers, is fully reflected in *Singapore: The Next Lap*,[54] that, according to Prime Minister Goh Chok Tong, "represents the hopes of a new generation of Singaporeans and their leaders". Unlike their exceptionally hardened and cheerless predecessors, who were preoccupied with creating "a rugged society", they are not even averse to spoiling Singaporeans a bit and letting them acquire graciousness and have some leisure and fun. They want to give Singapore "a more rounded personality". Soon after taking over as Prime Minister, in May 1991, Goh Chok Tong told this writer:

> In the past . . . we emphasised primarily the basics, relating to economics. That's unquestionably a very important aspect. But that's a one-dimensional aspect of a society's development. No. Having succeeded in fulfilling the basic needs, we have got to address the question: how do you make life more fulfilling for Singaporeans?[55]

According to *The Next Lap*, the Singapore of the future will be a modern city with world-class infrastructure and facilities, as well as a tropical island of fun and leisure. It will be a city that offers diversity and choice, a city with a rich variety of environments, a city of character and grace.[56]

In general terms, their different outlook and view of the Singapore of the future give them a special disposition to seek to improve the position of all ordinary Singaporeans.

Prime Minister Goh Chok Tong, talking about the changing position of the Malays in Singapore and the general problem of disparities, told this writer recently:

> In the past the Malay community felt that it had been lagging behind the others and that the government had not been doing enough to help them. Now they can see that the government is helping them and that they are making progress within the system. That gives them tremendous confidence that the system is not detrimental to their progress. I think this is the key difference today compared to the past. It is important to recognise that when one community is not doing as well as the others, tension will be created within the society.[57]

He added that it was important that each community felt that it was doing well for then they would want "to keep the system going". He saw it as a necessary precondition for the maintenance of a stable political order in Singapore.

Prime Minister Goh Chok Tong and his colleagues today have a different — more positive and optimistic — view of the Malays. They have been influenced by the progress achieved by the community during the 1980s. An indication of the progress achieved by the Malays during the ten-year period, 1981 to 1991, is given in Table 11. A prominent Malay professional told this writer recently:

> The attitudes of PAP leaders towards the Malay community have changed in a significant way during the last few years, especially after the second-generation leaders under Prime Minister Goh Chok Tong assumed power in late 1990. The Malays are no more viewed, to the extent as before, as the

Table 7: Working Persons Aged Fifteen and over by Monthly Income and Ethnic Group, 1980 and 1990

(in per cent)

Monthly income ($)	Chinese	Malays	Indians	Others
Below 500				
1980	60.2	81.7	68.7	31.9
1990	6.9	9.4	17.6	57.4
500 – 999				
1980	26.6	15.7	20.2	12.7
1990	36.8	47.8	38.9	16.1
1,000 – 1,499				
1980	6.7	1.8	4.8	7.4
1990	24.5	27.0	21.7	4.5
1,500 – 1,999				
1980	2.9	0.5	2.1	5.8
1990	12.4	9.4	9.5	3.0
2,000 – 2,999				
1980	2.1	0.2	2.3	9.9
1990	10.2	4.6	6.8	4.4
3,000 and over				
1980	1.5	0.1	1.9	32.3
1990	9.8	1.8	5.5	14.6
Average, $				
1980	595	388	568	2,307
1990	1,497	1,049	1,195	1,408

Source: *Singapore Census of Population, 1990*, Table 13, p. 17.

source of a variety of problems and as being incapable of change and progress. They have now begun to be viewed as capable of modernisation through education and acquisition of skills. But in this regard, the attitudes of Chinese Singaporeans in general have not changed all that much; most of them still hold the old negative views, stereotypes and prejudices.

In the past, the Malays were viewed as a fringe of the Singapore society that did not have a great deal to contribute to the modern, dynamic and prosperous Singapore. But now the PAP leaders have begun to look at us as a part of the mainstream of the modern Singapore society.[58]

Table 8: *Number of Households by Type of Dwelling, 1980 and 1990*

(in thousands)

	Chinese 1980	Chinese 1990	Malays 1980	Malays 1990	Indians 1980	Indians 1990
Private houses	33.1	40.2	1.4	1.0	3.6	3.6
HDB/JTC dwellings*						
1 and 2 room	77.3	41.6	18.5	5.8	7.3	6.1
3 room	124.1	176.6	19.7	40.7	7.4	15.1
4 room or more	53.1	213.9	5.0	32.5	3.9	18.5
Others	4.5	3.9	0.3	0.1	0.5	0.5
Other public flats	5.3	8.9	1.9	0.5	1.8	0.9
Condominiums and private flats	9.2	23.9	0.2	0.3	0.9	1.5
Others	66.0	14.8	13.3	1.0	8.7	1.8

Source: *Singapore Census of Population, 1990,* Key Indicators of the Population, p. xv.
*Housing Development Board and Jurong Town Council Dwellings

Table 9: *Students by Level of Education, 1980 and 1990*

(in thousands)

	Chinese 1980	Chinese 1990	Malays 1980	Malays 1990	Indians 1980	Indians 1990
Pre-Primary	39.3	40.4	6.5	10.5	2.4	4.1
Primary	220.7	194.7	48.9	43.9	17.9	18.4
Secondary	129.1	135.2	25.6	20.3	10.5	9.8
Upper Secondary	24.4	54.1	1.8	4.6	1.9	3.1
University	6.3	20.6	0.2	0.8	0.4	1.1

Source: *Singapore Census of Population, 1990,* Key Indicators of the Population, p. xvi.

Table 10: *Occupational Distribution of Workforce, 1980 and 1990*

(in per cent)

	Chinese 1980	Chinese 1990	Malays 1980	Malays 1990	Indians 1980	Indians 1990
Professional and technical	12.2	17.3	6.0	9.7	11.3	12.5
Administrative and managerial	6.8	10.0	0.7	1.1	6.4	5.8
Clerical	14.9	13.8	9.9	15.4	11.2	11.7
Sales and services	15.2	14.5	12.0	14.0	15.9	14.8
Agriculture and fishery	1.8	0.3	1.0	0.3	0.5	0.1
Production work	42.8	39.7	67.8	57.0	47.2	50.4

Source: *Singapore Census & Population, 1990*, Key Indicators of the Population, p. xiii

The basic approach of the government in its attempts to ameliorate the situation has been, firstly, to focus on education and skills as a means of improving the position of the lower classes, and secondly, to assist the communities that have lagged behind in dealing with the problems themselves. This approach of the government is influenced by its uncompromising commitment to a meritocratic system in Singapore and its view that the social engineering and attitudinal changes required to make significant progress in ameliorating the disparities are best attempted through the communities themselves. The government is entirely opposed to any programmes of positive discrimination in favour of one group or another as they believe that these would conflict with their own commitment to meritocracy; they have been pursuaded in this regard not only by the innate advantage of the meritocratic principle, but also by the experience of Third World countries where such programmes have created inter-ethnic disharmony as well as considerable corruption and nepotism, and have largely failed to achieve their objectives.

They also see a practical political problem in pursuing programmes of positive discrimination. Prime Minister Goh Chok Tong told this writer recently:

You know the Chinese constitute some 76 per cent of the population and the Malays form only fifteen to sixteen per cent. So if you have positive discrimination to help the Malay community, the poorer Chinese, who are at the same economic level as the poor Malays, will argue that they too need positive discrimination. This group in absolute numbers is bigger than the Malays who need help. Once you make one group happy through positive discrimination, you will make another group unhappy. So the best policy is to treat all communities on an equal basis and then find ways to help the disadvantaged chiefly through community-based self-help programmes.[59]

Table 11: *Progress Achieved by Malays, 1981 and 1991*

(in per cent)

	1981	1991
1. Families in HDB flats	72.0	97.2
In 1- and 2-room flats	30.3	6.4
In 3-room flats	32.9	49.1
In 4-room flats	8.3	41.7
2. Ownership of dwelling	49.9	94.1
HDB	53.3	95.0
Private	35.3	90.0
Other	41.3	54.5
3. Able to use English	65.8	73.0
Able to read newspapers	86.7	91.7
Using English at home	2.3	5.4
4. Pursuing secondary education	11.7	25.4
Pursuing higher secondary education	2.4	4.3
In universities	0.2	0.6
5. Professionals, entrepreneurs, managers and administrators	6.8	11.0
6. Ownership of		
Refrigerator	86.7	98.4
Colour television	11.1	98.8
Washing machine	10.9	83.0
Video	–	81.0

Source: Department of Statistics

He added that the problem of disparities related not only to the Malays:

> Within the Chinese community there are large numbers of Chinese-educated Singaporeans who too have a problem. These are intelligent people. They believe that they are educated in the wrong language medium. They cannot speak or write English as well as the English-educated. Because the language of administration is English, they feel disadvantaged. They too believe that the government is not helping them enough.[60]

Prime Minister Goh Chok Tong believes that the surest solution to the problem lies in the promotion and enhancement of education and skills among those who have lagged behind. In this regard, he is of the view that not a great deal can be achieved by efforts that are organised and managed by the government itself through its own bureaucracy. He firmly believes that the different communities themselves have to play a vital role. He recently explained to this writer that the government "can give a helping hand, but the change in attitude has to be effected by the communities themselves. We can provide facilities, including finances".[61] He added:

> To be effective, the appeal to those who need help must come from the communities, from their leaders. The communities would operate the programmes with a passion, a deep commitment, that the bureaucracy cannot. You must have that. If you leave them to the government, they would be run by a bureaucracy which can design schemes but lack the emotional ties to draw out the people to take advantage of them. We believe in getting the successful to help the less able in the community.[62]

In this regard, Prime Minister Goh Chok Tong and his colleagues, following on the successful experience of MENDAKI, the self-help organisation of the Malay community (*Majlis Pendidikan Anak-Anak Islam* — Council for the Education of Muslim

Children), formed in 1982, have supported the formation of similar organisations by the Indian and Chinese communities. Immediately following the formation of MENDAKI, many Indians had come to feel that since the overall position of their community had not been greatly better than that of the Malay community, they should have been given the same sort of special assistance by the government as the Malays and that they too should have been allowed to form a MENDAKI-like organisation of their own. However, based on the attitudes of the PAP rulers then and their lack of any special concern about ethnic disparities — except in the case of the indigenous Malays — the government had neither offered the Indians the necessary assistance nor the permission to form a MENDAKI-like organisation.

But, starting from the late 1980s, as we noted earlier, Goh Chok Tong and his second-generation colleagues began to concern themselves more seriously with the issue of ethnic disparities and considered it as one of their special objectives to attempt to deal with the problem. In this regard, they sought to help improve the position not only of the Malays, but also that of the Indians as well as the Chinese-speaking. In August 1991, with the active assistance of the government, the Indians established the Singapore Indian Development Association, SINDA, to tackle the serious educational and socio-economic problems facing the Indian community and build "a well-educated, resilient and confident community of Indians" in Singapore. Less than a year later, in May 1992, the Chinese community similarly established the Chinese Development Assistance Council, CDAC. The result has been that, since 1992, the Malays, the Chinese and the Indians all have come to have their own separate voluntary organisations with the specific purpose to promote educational and socio-economic progress within their respective communities.

1. MENDAKI
The best organised is the Malay organisation, MENDAKI, which was established in 1982. Dr Ahmad Mattar, who was then a minister in the PAP government, had played an important role in its formation. Its founders were in agreement that "the pace of

economic and socio-cultural development would not improve without heavy emphasis on education for young Muslims. Education was the launch-pad for all other progress."[63] This emphasis was reflected in the organisation's activities which, until 1989, were entirely related to promoting education and higher educational attainment among the Malays.

In May 1989, MENDAKI was especially encouraged by First Deputy Prime Minister Goh Chok Tong to extend its responsibilities to deal with a wide variety of other problems facing the Malay community and to strengthen its organisation and activities. Promotion of education and skills among Malays, however, remained one of its key activities. Its widened responsibilities now included assisting Malays in achieving economic progress so that the gap between them and the others could be narrowed in the future. Reflecting the specially strong commitment of Goh Chok Tong and his colleagues to the Asianisation of Singapore, it also committed itself to strengthening among the Malays "values consistent with Islamic teachings in order to contribute to wholesome family and social and cultural values".[64]

MENDAKI has since its foundation been closely associated with the PAP government. Its board of directors is headed by a senior Malay member of the government and its chief executive officer is either a public servant seconded by the government or a person acceptable to the government. The government provides considerable financial and other assistance; for the remainder of its budget it depends on regular voluntary contributions by Malays/Muslims and others. Its highly subsidised activities and services include the following:

Education
a. Weekend tuition scheme, home tuition scheme, education clinics and revision classes.
b. Scholarships, educational awards and interest-free study loans. Computer appreciation courses.
c. Child and family development talks, seminars and workshops, including programmes for pre-schoolers.

Economic Development
a. Public economic education programme.
b. Talks and workshops on career opportunities and development.
c. Seminars and workshops on skills and entrepreneurial development.
d. Assistance in identifying economic opportunities for the community especially where Malays/Muslims have comparative advantages.

Social and Cultural Affairs
a. Study on low-income families and possible assistance programme.
b. Liaison and work with various agencies on drug and drug-related problems in the Malay/Muslim community.
c. Study on high divorce rates and single parents in the Malay/Muslim community and ways of tackling the issue.
d. Coordination and assistance in selected aspects of Malay cultural activities.

2. SINDA

SINDA too is closely associated with the PAP government. Indian members of parliament from the PAP are fully involved in its management and activities. It is headed by a senior, highly experienced public servant. It is administered by a public servant seconded by the government, who holds the position of chief executive officer. It too depends on the government for financial and other assistance, though it raises considerable amounts of money from the Indian community in the form of donations and regular monthly contributions.

From the beginning, its objectives and activities have covered the two areas of education and welfare. Its special emphasis on education has emanated from the 1991 Report of the Action Committee on Indian Education which identified the serious problem of educational underperformance by Indian pupils, especially in mathematics and science. It is committed to helping Indians "to achieve parity in educational attainment with the national average at every landmark examination, by the year 2010".[65] In this regard, its activities include:

a. Tuition classes in mathematics, science and English, starting with underachievers, conducted by professional teachers, using specially prepared instructional materials.
b. Parent outreach activities to educate and motivate parents to play a positive role in their children's education. Project *Vidya* to nurture the talents and capabilities of students of high calibre.
c. Promotion of pre-school learning, technical education and computer education.
d. Tertiary Mentor Scheme.

It also offers support through scholarships and bursaries. As to welfare, it seeks "to strengthen the family unit and build a cohesive and caring community" through the following programmes: Family Service Centre, Family Life Education, Children and Youth Development and Voluntary Development. It also runs counselling and referral services for needy families.

3. CDAC

Prime Minister Goh Chok Tong, as the patron of CDAC, appointed its fifteen-member board of directors, headed by Wong Kan Seng, a Cabinet minister. Its chief executive officer is a public servant seconded by the government who administers its activities. For its funding, it depends on the government and the community.

Its activities relate entirely to the promotion of education and skills among the Chinese. It was not especially formed to assist the Chinese-speaking but its services are mostly used by the Chinese-speaking to improve their position. It started with a low-fee tuition programme in Chinese, English and mathematics "to help students improve their studies and to cope with the subjects with more confidence". It also has a variety of Skills Training Programmes to assist low-skilled and low-income workers to upgrade their skills and improve their earning capabilities. These enable low-income and low-skilled workers to attend a variety of upgrading courses offered at the Institute of Technical Education and other similar institutions.

Based on the significant progress made by the Malay community through the activities of MENDAKI during the last twelve years,

Prime Minister Goh Chok Tong and his colleagues believe that there is no reason why the Indians and the Chinese-speaking too should not be able to improve their position considerably with assistance from their own community organisations over the next decade or so. In any case, with regard to the Chinese-speaking the problem of disparities is seen as being only a temporary, short-term one. Firstly, expanding trade and the economic relationship with China have created immense new opportunities for the Chinese-speaking. Secondly, they are a part of the dominant Chinese majority and as such their dissatisfaction with the gap between them and the English-speaking does not have the same serious implications for the management of ethnicity as that of the indigenous Malays and the Indians. Finally, since English has been the sole medium of instruction at all levels of education for some ten years now, the Chinese-speaking are a fast declining group; in 20 years or so few of them will be left.

In the case of the Indians, even though they constitute only a small part of the population, the government is now worried about the damaging impact of the disparities between them and the others on the overall ethnic environment and relationships in Singapore. Indians are divided into a large variety of speech communities, each with its own distinctive ethnic identity. The problem of educational underperformance and low incomes is restricted chiefly to the Tamil-speaking, who constitute more than half of the Indian population. Members of other Indian speech communities have been doing well and they do not have any fear of falling behind the Chinese. A prominent Indian leader of the PAP told this writer recently: "The problem of the Indians is largely that of the Tamils. Non-Tamil Indians are essentially doing very well and they do not face any special problems."[66]

According to him, what is desperately needed among the Tamils is a Tamil Kemal Ataturk who could modernise the community and prepare them for fuller participation in the modern and thriving Singapore of today and tomorrow. He is pessimistic about the future as he has doubts if even a Kemal Ataturk could achieve a great deal of success in creating a revolution among the Tamils. Tamil political culture, behaviour and style are not easily given to radical change and reform. Their own traditional leadership, as well as the Indian Tamil leaders (virtually treated as demigods and worshipped by the Singaporean Tamils) who visit them frequently, tend to be preoccupied with glorifying and romanticising the past greatness of the Tamils, their language and culture and their way of life. On their visits to Singapore the Tamil leaders from Tamil Nadu in India even poke fun at and deprecate the ways and values of the Singaporean Chinese and Malays. The main theme of their speeches in Singapore is the greatness and superiority of the Tamils. According to the PAP leader quoted above, the result is that many Singapore Tamils, especially those at the bottom

> ... tend to live in a world of make-believe, of their superiority and greatness as a community. They are deterred from taking a realistic look at themselves and their community. They have become recalcitrant and strongly resistant to change. They have developed an excessive fear of losing their distinctive Tamil identity, in ways similar to that shown by the Malays. What constitutes their identity is often pushed to ridiculous extremes and it creates a deep antipathy to any change and modernisation.[67]

Beyond their attempts to ameliorate the problem of disparities between ethnic segments that we considered above, Prime Minister Goh Chok Tong and his colleagues have begun to view the multi-racial character of Singapore's population as a key asset in their quest for continuing economic growth and prosperity. It is maintained that Singapore had come into existence, and it had developed and prospered historically, as a multi-racial and multi-cultural entity. This was the basis on which the British had been able to build up Singapore as the premier centre of trade in Southeast Asia. Recognising that crucial reality, the PAP rulers have sought to maintain that character of Singapore since 1959 when they first assumed power. For this purpose, more recently, they have even gone to the extent of encouraging migration from the countries around Singapore.

It is now argued that the multi-racial and multi-cultural character of Singapore, its special asset, should be taken advantage of to give each of the major ethnic components of its population — the Malays, the Chinese and the Indians — a special economic base of their own. A senior member of the government told this writer recently:

> It [Singapore's multi-racial populace] gives us an easy understanding of a variety of peoples, those in East Asia through our Chinese, those in the South Asian subcontinent through our Indians and others, and those in the Malay world of Southeast Asia through our indigenous Malays. That understanding gives us a special access to those regions... We can successfully and profitably deal with a variety of Asian peoples and build up mutually beneficial trade and other economic relationships with them. If we were all Chinese in Singapore, it would not have been that easy for Prime Minister Goh to lead the large group of Singaporeans that is in India today to create a new era of close economic cooperation between Singapore and India.[68]

The idea is that Chinese Singaporeans have facilitated the plugging of Singapore to the Chinese world of East Asia and by doing that they have created substantial new opportunities for the Chinese-speaking to improve their position and prosper. Similarly, Indian Singaporeans are beginning to facilitate the plugging of Singapore to the vast markets of the Indian subcontinent, which will inevitably give them a special place and role in the expanding economy of Singapore in the future. It is the expectation of the government that the Singaporean Malays will soon come to play a similarly profitable role in specially plugging Singapore to its large, and increasingly prosperous, Malay neighbours, Indonesia and Malaysia.

Maintaining a National Consensus on the Management of Ethnicity

Prime Minister Goh Chok Tong and his young colleagues in the government face an especially serious challenge in establishing and maintaining a national consensus with regard to the modifications in the application of the founding principle of a multi-racial cultural democracy that they consider necessary. As we noted before at the beginning of Chapter 3, when the first-generation PAP rulers devised their approach to the management of ethnicity during the period from 1959 to 1965, they did not have to worry excessively about consulting the Chinese and the Indians and ensuring that their own ideas necessarily conformed to the wishes of these ethnic groups. They had to concern themselves chiefly with the views and feelings of the indigenous Malays and Singapore's powerful neighbours, Malaysia and Indonesia, and ensure that their approach to and their management of ethnicity did not excessively displease them. Prime Minister Lee Kuan Yew and his colleagues had then devised the "national consensus" on the issue of their approach to and management of ethnicity themselves and delivered it to the people of Singapore.

Today the situation has changed dramatically. Singapore is now allowed to function as a greatly more open society, thanks to the personal political inclinations and style of Prime Minister Goh Chok Tong and the will of its citizens. Its different peoples, benefiting from the spectacular social, economic and educational progress of the past quarter century, have begun to assert themselves as citizens of a "democracy that works". Of course, floodgates have not been opened. But clearly, Singaporeans' excessive fear of government has begun to disappear and increasing numbers of them are seeking greater participation for themselves in the polity. They want their Confucian rulers to consult them more and to rule Singapore more and more with their consent. Thus, today Prime Minister Goh Chok Tong and his government can no more design and deliver a national approach with regard to the management of ethnicity without the participation and consent of their peoples, representing a variety of ethnic groups.

The problem for them has been further accentuated by the increasing openness of public discussion and debate on sensitive ethnic issues, often encouraged and initiated by the PAP political rulers themselves. Community leaders from the different ethnic segments, and even many PAP members of parliament, show little hesitation in publicly speaking on behalf of their own respective communities and seeking to promote their interests.

Today the government can neither still these voices nor can it afford to ignore them altogether. It has no choice but to respond to them and devise policies on contentious ethnic issues and defend them publicly.

The increasing resurgence among the Chinese with regard to their role and status as the dominant majority and their demand to strengthen their distinctive identity, culture and heritage, and the resultant heightening of suspicion and fear among the non-Chinese have made the challenge for Prime Minister Goh Chok Tong and his colleagues much more critical. They cannot afford to lose sight of the fact that the unique success of the first-generation PAP rulers in this regard was based on an extremely careful balancing, with exemplary ethnic sensitivity and fairmindedness, of the often conflicting dreams and desires of the diverse populace of Singapore.

In this regard, it has been unfortunate that during the last three years the team of second-generation rulers, headed by Prime Minister Goh Chok Tong, has been considerably weakened. In late 1991, following the general elections, two pre-eminent members of the team, Dr Tony Tan and S Dhanabalan, chose to leave the government for personal reasons. Within a year, the Prime Minister was to make the sad announcement that his two Deputy Prime Ministers and key members of his already depleted team, Ong Teng Cheong and Brigadier-General Lee Hsien Loong, had been inflicted with cancer. Not long afterwards, two other members of the team, Dr Ahmad Mattar (the sole Malay member of the team) and Dr Yeo Ning Hong, too decided to leave the government. With the recent election of Ong Teng Cheong as the President of Singapore, Prime Minister Goh Chok Tong today heads a government which consists almost entirely of younger PAP leaders who are the products of post-independence Singapore.

Prime Minister Goh Chok Tong has always enjoyed the fullest confidence and respect of all the different ethnic groups as a caring, gentle and fairminded national leader. His non-combative, consultative political style is especially suited to the aspirations of Singaporeans of today who are greatly more affluent and politically sophisticated and better-educated than in the past. However, despite Goh Chok Tong's own high standing and personal popularity, minorities have tended to worry about his government and its policies. Their worries relate to his young colleagues in the government who did not themselves experience the intense ethnic contradictions of the 1950s and the early 1960s and the accommodations made at the time. It is feared that they may not possess the necessary ethnic sensitivity and the patience to deal with the different ethnic segments with understanding and evenhandedness and be able to create and sustain a national consensus on the management of ethnic diversity.

On the whole, however, such fears can easily be exaggerated by some in moments of anger, powerlessness and frustration. Based on the unmatched record of PAP leaders, representing two different generations, one can have nothing but optimism about the future. The momentum of change and progress in Singapore — affluence, modernisation and education — is such that there is little scope for utterly irrational and destructive chauvinism to reassert itself in its maddening way and threaten the multi-racial foundations of today's Singapore. Moreover, the practical sense displayed by Singaporeans during the past quarter century does suggest that they can be relied upon not to succumb to appeals to ethnicity in the future.

Notes

1. Interview with a top-ranking second-generation leader of government, Singapore, January 1983.
2. Interview with a top-ranking leader of government, Singapore, January 1994.
3. Interview with a top-ranking second-generation leader of government, Singapore, November 1992.
4. Interview with a PAP member of parliament, Singapore, December 1990.
5. Interview with a top-ranking second-generation leader of government, Singapore, January 1989.
6. *Ibid.*
7. Interview with a top-ranking Malay leader of government, Singapore, December 1988.
8. Leslie Fong, "Domestic Politics", in Tan Teng Lang (editor), *Singapore: The Year in Review, 1990*, Institute of Policy Studies, Singapore 1991, pp. 9–10.

9. Interview with a prominent Malay professional and intellectual who has been actively involved with the community, Singapore, September 1993.
10. Interview with S Rajaratnam, Singapore, December 1982.
11. *Ibid.*
12. Interview with a top-ranking leader of government, Singapore, January 1994.
13. Interview with Goh Chok Tong, Singapore, May 1991.
14. Interview with a senior first-generation leader of government, Singapore, May 1992.
15. Interview with Goh Chok Tong, Singapore, May 1991.
16. *Ibid.*
17. *Ibid.*
18. *Ibid.*
19. Interview with a prominent second-generation leader of government, Singapore, December 1992.
20. *The Straits Times*, 2 December 1992.
21. *The Straits Times*, 6 March 1992.
22. *Ibid.*
23. This description is based on interviews with two top-ranking second-generation leaders of the PAP, Singapore, November–December 1992.
24. Interview with S Rajaratnam, Singapore, 1982.
25. Interview with a top-ranking second-generation leader of government, Singapore, December 1992.
26. *Ibid.*
27. Leslie Fong, "Domestic Politics", in Tan Teng Lang (editor), *Singapore: The Year in Review, 1990*, Institute of Policy Studies, Singapore 1991, p. 10.
28. *The Straits Times*, 17 September 1991.
29. *Ibid.*
30. *The Straits Times*, 18 September 1991.
31. *Ibid.*
32. Commenting on the speech by Deputy Prime Minister Ong Teng Cheong, on 22 September, Prime Minister Goh Chok Tong said, "I would rate Mr Ong as representing the conservative, Chinese section of the PAP." *The Straits Times*, 23 September 1991.
33. *The Straits Times*, 23 September 1991.
34. *Ibid.*
35. *Ibid.*
36. *Ibid.*
37. *The Straits Times*, 23 September 1991.
38. *Ibid.*
39. *Ibid.*
40. *Ibid.*
41. Interview with a senior member of government, Singapore, April 1993.
42. Interview with a leader of the PAP, Singapore, January 1994.
43. *Ibid.*

44 *The Straits Times*, 27 September 1991.
45 Interview with Dr Ow Chin Hock, then a Senior Lecturer in Economics at the National University of Singapore, Singapore, May 1992.
46 Interview with a prominent leader of the Chinese-speaking, Singapore, May 1992.
47 *Ibid.*
48 *Ibid.*
49 Interview with a group of editors and senior journalists of Chinese language newspapers in Singapore, Singapore, January 1994.
50 Interview with a PAP leader, Singapore, December 1992.
51 Interview with a Chinese-speaking leader of the PAP, Singapore, January 1994.
52 Interview with a pre-eminent leader of the present government, Singapore, mid-1983.
53 Interview with a pre-eminent second-generation leader of government, Singapore, January 1983.
54 *Singapore: The Next Lap*, Singapore 1991. Produced by the second-generation leaders, soon after Goh Chok Tong took over as Prime Minister of Singapore.
55 Interview with Goh Chok Tong, Singapore, May 1991.
56 *Singapore: The Next Lap*, Singapore 1991, p. 77.
57 Interview with Goh Chok Tong, Singapore, January 1994.
58 Interview with a prominent Malay professional, Singapore, September 1993.
59 Interview with Goh Chok Tong, Singapore, January 1994.
60 *Ibid.*
61 *Ibid.*
62 *Ibid.*
63 MENDAKI, *Making the Difference: Ten Years of MENDAKI*, Singapore 1992, p. 50.
64 *Ibid.*
65 SINDA, *1991 Report of the Action Committee on Indian Education*, Singapore 1991.
66 Interview with a prominent Indian leader of the PAP, Singapore, December 1993.
67 *Ibid.*
68 Interview with a senior member of government, Singapore, January 1994.

INDEX

A

Action Committee on Indian Education   148, 158
All Party Committee on Chinese Education   19, 50
Alliance, the   12
Asian values   60–62, 65, 77, 78, 100, 122
Asianising Singapore   6, 64, 65, 69, 77, 85, 87, 93–97, 102, 113, 121
Association of Southeast Asian Nations (ASEAN)   66

B

Barisan Sosialis   11, 15, 40–42, 48, 67
Bible Knowledge   73
bilingualism   56–58, 74
bumiputra   13, 16, 17, 23–25, 29, 43, 45, 88, 107

C

Chan Heng Chee   42
Chiam See Tong   119
Chinese Development Assistance Council (CDAC)   130, 146
Chinese Press Club   122
Chinese Singapore   5–7, 10, 17, 96, 117, 127, 131, 134
Chineseness of Singapore   4, 6, 7, 9, 29, 38, 94, 104, 105, 107, 116, 117, 131, 133, 134
Chineseness of the Chinese   11, 12, 64, 75, 85, 94, 105, 114, 117, 120, 121
communitarianism   84, 129
Confucian Ethics   73, 82
Confucianism   65, 73, 74, 81–83, 94, 118
Constitution of Malaya   13, 23
Constitution of Singapore   44
Constitutional Commission   27
core values   65, 78–80

cultural democracy   4–7, 18, 22, 24–30, 33–35, 38, 41, 44, 46–50, 53, 55, 62, 64, 66, 84, 94, 96, 97, 100, 110, 121, 134, 153

D

Dhanabalan, S   51, 154

F

Federation of Malaya   2, 9, 13
Federation of Malaysia   12, 13, 16, 18, 19, 41
Furnivall, J S   3

G

Goh Chok Tong   75, 77, 78, 84, 91–93, 95, 99–101, 103, 105, 106, 108–110, 112–117, 121, 125, 126, 135, 137–140, 143, 145–147, 149–155
Goh Keng Swee, Dr   69, 73

H

Ho Wing Meng   60
Housing and Development Board (HDB)   51, 52
Hsu Cho Yun   73

I

Indonesian "confrontation"   20
Islamic Religious Knowledge   73

J

Jeyaretnam, J B   69, 119

L

Lee Hsien Loong, Brigadier-General   72, 93, 108, 124, 154

Lee Kuan Yew   9, 10, 12, 15, 17, 38, 45, 49, 52, 53, 55–58, 61, 62, 65, 67, 69–71, 78, 83, 87, 89, 90, 99, 100, 103, 105, 106, 108, 118, 123–127, 134, 135, 153

M

Malay Convention   23
Malay/Muslim Development Congress   95
Malayan Communist Party   105
Malaysia   8, 10–21, 23–26, 29, 41–45, 66, 67, 78, 94, 95, 100, 107–109, 111, 135, 138, 152, 153
Malaysian Malaysia   12, 14, 25, 95
Mattar, Dr Ahmad   146, 154
MENDAKI   90–92, 130, 145–147, 150
Ministry of Culture   46, 50
Ministry of Education   50, 69

N

Nanyang University   68, 128, 136
national ideology   65, 78, 79, 83, 84, 106
National Ideology Forum   81

O

Ong Teng Cheong   104, 122–124, 126, 154
Ow Chin Hock, Dr   104

P

Pancasila   78

R

Rajaratnam S   29, 33, 46, 102, 111, 112, 119, 127
religious knowledge   65, 73–75
Religious Knowledge curriculum   65, 73, 74
Report of the Action Committee on Indian Education, 1991   148
Report on Moral Education, 1979   73

Report on the Ministry of Education 69
Rukunegara 78, 79

S

shared values 79–83
Singapore Indian Development Association (SINDA) 146, 148
Singapore United Malays National Organisation 23
Singaporean Singapore 10, 17, 29, 40, 109, 117, 134, 136
Speak Mandarin Campaign 64, 65, 68–73, 90, 94, 107
Special Assistance Plan (SAP) 65, 75–77
Stamford Raffles 1
Sukarno, General/President 66

T

Tan, Dr Tony 75, 154
Tanah Melayu 2, 13, 21, 24, 43, 110
Third China 5, 9, 17, 18, 29, 39, 40
Toh Chin Chye, Dr 48
Tunku Abdul Rahman 12, 13

U

United Malays National Organisation (UMNO) 12, 23

V

Vogel, Ezra F 77, 84

W

Wee Kim Wee 79
White Paper on Shared Values 81–83
Wong Kan Seng 124, 149
Workers' Party 69, 119

Y

Yeo, Brigadier-General George 81
Yeo Ning Hong, Dr 154